THE PRE-EXISTING CONDITION

THE PRE-EXISTING CONDITION

Innovative Solutions to America's Thorniest Healthcare Challenge

edited by
ROBERT GRABOYES AND CHARLES BLAHOUS

MERCATUS CENTER
George Mason University
Arlington, Virginia

ABOUT THE MERCATUS CENTER

The Mercatus Center at George Mason University is the world's premier university source for market-oriented ideas—bridging the gap between academic ideas and real-world problems.

A university-based research center, Mercatus advances knowledge about how markets work to improve people's lives by training graduate students, conducting research, and applying economics to offer solutions to society's most pressing problems.

Our mission is to generate knowledge and understanding of the institutions that affect the freedom to prosper and to find sustainable solutions that overcome the barriers preventing individuals from living free, prosperous, and peaceful lives. Founded in 1980, the Mercatus Center is located on George Mason University's Arlington campus.

www.mercatus.org

ACKNOWLEDGMENTS

The Mercatus Center gratefully acknowledges the financial support of the John Templeton Foundation for research on healthcare policy in the United States. Mercatus also wishes to thank the staff of e21—the economics portal of the Manhattan Institute for Policy Research—which was kind enough to publish the first-run exclusive for the individual essays. Diana Furchtgott-Roth, Preston Cooper, and Jared Meyer were all instrumental in disseminating the innovative solutions essays by featuring them as the "Story of the Day" at economics21.org and in the headline of e21's influential eBriefs.

978-1-942951-21-6 paperbound

978-1-942951-22-3 Kindle ebook

Mercatus Center at George Mason University
3434 Washington Blvd., 4th Floor
Arlington, VA 22201
703-993-4930

"Imagine an economy where people could follow their passions and their talent without having to worry that their children would not have health insurance, that if they had a child with diabetes who was bipolar or [if they had a] pre-existing medical condition in their family, that they would be job-locked. Under this bill, their entrepreneurial spirit will be unleashed."

—Nancy Pelosi, March 21, 2010,
speech from the House floor before the final vote on the Affordable Care Act

CONTENTS

PREFACE

How to finance care for individuals with pre-existing medical conditions has long been one of the thorniest, most challenging issues in healthcare policy. The Patient Protection and Affordable Care Act's solution was a vast, complex clockwork of individual and employer coverage mandates, guaranteed issue, modified community rating, multiple subsidies, and other provisions. As commentators spanning the political spectrum warned before the law's passage, this approach faces daunting logistical and financial hurdles.

In a new set of essays commissioned by the Mercatus Center at George Mason University, seven leading policy experts share innovative ideas on how to solve the pre-existing condition challenge. While their approaches exhibit differences as well as similarities, they are unified in their pursuit of a humane, equitable, fiscally sustainable solution to a conundrum that has driven and strained the entire post–World War II healthcare debate.

—The Editors

Robert Graboyes

CHANGING THE SUBJECT

The Patient Protection and Affordable Care Act's individual mandate is an intrusive, expensive, mechanistic device for expanding the number of people with insurance cards rather than for the more important goal of bringing better care to more people at lower cost year after year.

The best alternative to the individual mandate is technological innovation that makes people ask why on earth anyone ever thought a mandate was necessary. In contrast with the creeping pace of healthcare technology over the past 25 years, information technology has, in fact, brought better computing and telecommunications to more people at lower cost year after year.

In 1990, I knew one person with a mobile telephone. Today, there are 7 billion cell phones on earth—more than the number of toilets or toothbrushes. Residents of the humblest villages in the developing world carry phones more powerful than 1980s supercomputers. IT has gone from a luxury for the wealthy to universal coverage (to borrow a healthcare buzzword).

In contrast, healthcare technology has advanced only modestly since 1990. Why the difference? Put simply, a bipartisan consensus allowed IT to innovate while health care was mired in a furious, partisan debate over how to distribute fixed stocks of resources.

This can change.

THE DEBATE PROVOKES BITTER PARTISANSHIP

Since World War II, both Left and Right have battled over how best to allocate fixed quantities of doctors, hospitals, drugs, devices, and insurance dollars. Asked not long ago about the effects of the Affordable Care Act (ACA), I responded, "Some people get better coverage and others worse. It makes some people better off financially and others worse off. It likely improves health for some and worsens it for others. By none of these criteria do the winners clearly outnumber the losers. In sum, the law merely redistributes wealth and health at enormous cost."[1] The same would be true of proposals from the Right (e.g., high-risk pools, Medicaid block grants) and the Left (e.g., single-payer health care).

The ACA expands access to care by particular groups of individuals and for particular medical services. But the act does little to expand the supply of healthcare resources or, despite lip service in that direction, to improve the efficiency of delivery.

The individual mandate reflects one such distributive vision. Proposed alternatives reflect other visions. All are rife with winners and losers. Whether a particular scheme "works" depends on who you are, what you want, and when you want it.

THE DEBATE SUBORDINATES TECHNOLOGICAL ADVANCES

With the public and policymakers focused almost exclusively on the distribution of care, healthcare technology policy has meandered counterproductively in the shadows.

My 2014 study "Fortress and Frontier in American Health Care" argued that medicine has been consigned to a "Fortress," characterized by paternalism for patients and protectionism for providers.[2] The Food and Drug Administration, for example, is institutionally biased toward excessive caution. If the FDA releases a drug that kills 100 people, alarms sound and careers crash and burn. But if the FDA fails to release a drug that could

---

1. "Obamacare's Latest Challenge," interview with Robert Graboyes, *Outlook* 12, no. 4 (CoBank, April 2015).

2. Robert F. Graboyes, "Fortress and Frontier in American Health Care" (Mercatus Research, Mercatus Center at George Mason University, Arlington, VA, October 2014).

have saved 10,000 people, its inaction carries few penalties. Hence, the FDA will almost always steer toward risk-aversion.

Inaction or sluggish action has a compounding effect. In any innovative sector, one innovation leads to others. Slowing the rollout of a particular product hampers future progress in two ways: First, if the introduction of a new drug is delayed five years, spinoffs will likely also be delayed five years. Second, if the introduction of a new drug is delayed five years, some serendipitous interactions that would have yielded spinoffs will never occur, and the potential ideas will never see the light.

Excessive caution has also hampered innovation in other areas of health care. It has slowed the advent of genomic medicine, the use of telemedicine, the establishment of more efficient hospitals, the creative use of non-physician medical labor, and the development of more up-to-date medical education. Privacy and security concerns unnecessarily paralyze lines of inquiry. Most of all, excessive caution has limited the role patients and consumers can play in managing their own health.

The aversion to provider competition is as powerful as the aversion to patient risk. Once again, the focus on distribution allows cronyism to go nearly unchecked in health care. Hospitals employ certificate-of-need laws to stave off potential competitors. Physicians similarly use restrictions on professional licensure, nonphysician scope of practice, medical school slots, and telemedicine to do the same. Insurers enjoy cozy relationships with state insurance commissioners. All these restrictions straddle the line between disinterested risk-aversion and deeply interested cronyism.

The present-day cascade of new technologies—genomics, 3-D printing, nanotechnology, wireless telemetry, artificial intelligence, big data—offers a chance to replicate in health care the dynamism we have seen in information technology over the past generation. But until we shift the healthcare debate away from its monomaniacal focus on distributive issues (i.e., conflicting insurance plans), healthcare innovation will remain in the doldrums.

THE DEBATE SKEWS TECHNOLOGICAL PROGRESS

The focus on distribution does not merely result in neglect and slowing technological progress. The insurance schemes also skew medical technology in particular directions.

An individual mandate (or a high-risk pool, a single-payer system, etc.) mechanistically offers to cover a particular array of medical goods and services. Medicare's reimbursement methodology is perhaps the starkest example, though it is mirrored in other forms of health insurance. Medicare excludes whole classes of goods and services from coverage: particular drugs and devices, time spent in email and telephone communication, telemedicine visits, purchases from international providers, experimental treatments. Limiting the flow of dollars in these ways shapes the sorts of goods and services provided, as well as research and development on newer modes of treatment.

The slow acceptance of new forms of health care unnecessarily heightens costs and risks, discouraging entrepreneurs and venture capitalists. After desiccating the capital markets for healthcare research and development, the government often seeks to fill the gap.

The ACA, for example, established the Centers for Medicare & Medicaid Services Innovation Center to serve as a clearinghouse for healthcare payment and delivery innovations. The central problem with the center is encapsulated in a recent article in the *Atlantic*. Titled "Why Experts Reject Creativity," the caption reads, "People think they like creativity. But teachers, scientists, and executives are biased against new ways of thinking."[3] And by their very nature, public-sector incubators rely on teachers, scientists, and executives.

THE IT DIFFERENCE

The explosive advancement of IT came from public policies that denied those insiders—teachers, scientists, and executives—veto power over innovation. These policies unleashed the uncredentialed genius that led to Apple and BlackBerry.

If the federal government had maintained its grip on ARPANET post-1990, the Internet today would look nothing like the miraculous world of Siri, GPS, Skype, Translator, Street View, Uber, Twitter, and so forth. If a Federal Department of Apps (FDA?) had maintained oversight over innovation, the new technologies would be few in number, high in cost, and

3. Derek Thompson, "Why Experts Reject Creativity," *Atlantic*, October 10, 2014, http://www.theatlantic.com/business/archive/2014/10/why-new-ideas-fail/381275/.

mediocre in function. And we would today be arguing about how best to distribute scarce IT resources.

Bringing computers, cell phones, and software to the world did not require an individual mandate or any other redistributive scheme. Universal coverage, the fantasy of healthcare reformers, became reality in IT within 25 years. And this was precisely because innovators could focus on creation of the new rather than on distribution of the old.

CONCLUSION

It would be naïve to think that the debate over distribution will suddenly give way to a debate over how best to unleash innovation. But it's desirable to begin shifting public discourse in that direction. Around 1990, remarkably, a bipartisan consensus emerged in Congress to unleash the unknown potential of the Internet by allowing consumers to take risks and denying IT producers protection from market forces. As a result, connectivity changed global society for the better, in a way that was an achievement of neither the political Left nor the political Right. And it mostly emerged spontaneously from markets, not from mandates.

The same option is open to health care, if only we choose to take it.

Douglas Holtz-Eakin

MARKET INCENTIVES FOR BROADER COVERAGE

The Patient Protection and Affordable Care Act (ACA) is a mandate-driven, regulation-heavy piece of legislation with the objective (among other goals) of insuring Americans with pre-existing conditions. Simply repealing the ACA would not result in insuring this group. This raises an important question: What *is* the conservative health policy approach to pre-existing conditions?

One answer is a two-pronged strategy that uses different tools to address pre-existing conditions in the current population and pre-existing conditions in the future. These approaches have the additional virtue that they not only provide insurance coverage but also infuse the market with incentives for better health care.

DEALING WITH PRE-EXISTING CONDITIONS IN THE FUTURE

Policymakers should begin by anticipating that pre-existing conditions will arise. In this case, the key is better incentives. Specifically, if a person buys insurance—in whatever market (individual, small group, employer, etc.)—and *stays* continuously covered—again, in whatever market—then no insurance company may "medically underwrite" the individual (i.e., evaluate him or her for pre-existing conditions). The individual must be treated as a healthy policyholder.

What happens? First, there is a tremendous incentive for young (and on average healthier) individuals to buy insurance. This brings cheap risks into the pool, and provides a way for the young to lock in relatively low premiums over their lifetimes. Insurers, on the other hand, now have to compete by providing a high-value policy (low premiums, high benefits) in a pool that contains a mixture of risks, instead of competing by excluding risks. The results are more competition and coverage for pre-existing conditions. Healthcare incentives are improved as well. If a young person buys an individual policy, there is a great possibility that the insurer will be responsible for bills many years into the future. Instead of making actuarial calculations based on a one year snapshot, insurers will look forward and recognize the payoff from investing in preventive services, lifestyle interventions, and seemingly costly cures (e.g., Sovaldi, the hepatitis C cure). In short, the insurance market competition will deliver incentives to *avoid* future "pre-existing" conditions.

DEALING WITH PRE-EXISTING CONDITIONS IN THE PRESENT

For those whose pre-existing conditions currently price them out of the insurance market, one solution is providing high-risk pools. This strategy recognizes that if the ratio of health costs to an individual's income is too high, then the right response is *not* to regulate every insurance product ("essential benefits"), every sales practice ("guaranteed issue"), and every price ("community rating"). The answer is to subsidize that individual, but retain the dynamism and flexibility of a private market.

High-risk pools are vehicles for subsidies where needed. Historically, states charter a high-risk pool and its board contracts with an insurance company to collect premiums and pay claims and administer the program on a day-to-day basis. (Most high-risk pools have been nonprofits, but there is no reason not to run a for-profit pool that has sharper incentives for claims adjustment.) The pools typically offer benefits that are comparable to those of basic private plans. The insurance generally costs more than regular individual insurance; it is made affordable through subsidies.

THE PATIENT CARE ACT

The approaches described here are far from theoretical. The Patient Choice, Affordability, Responsibility, and Empowerment (Patient CARE) Act proposed by Senators Richard Burr, Orrin Hatch, and Tom Coburn in January 2014 (and proposed again by Burr, Hatch, and Representative Fred Upton in January 2015) uses these approaches quite successfully, according to analysis from the Center for Health and Economy.[1] Specifically, the act would repeal the requirements for guaranteed issue under the ACA and replace them with requirements for guaranteed renewability. Individuals would have to maintain continuous insurance coverage in order to avoid being charged higher premiums based on health status. In the first year of implementation, there would be an open enrollment period during which all individuals would be guaranteed that they would be issued health insurance without regard to health status. At the same time, the Patient CARE Act would give states the authority to set up federally funded high-risk insurance pools.

CONCLUSION

There is nothing about health insurance markets that requires a mandate-heavy, regulatory approach to solving the problem of pre-existing conditions. Nor is there anything about pre-existing conditions that precludes an approach other than the ACA. The answer is a strategy that uses different tools to address pre-existing conditions in the current population and pre-existing conditions in the future. This strategy has the virtue of providing insurance coverage while also infusing the market with incentives for better health care.

---

1. "The Patient Choice, Affordability, Responsibility, and Empowerment Act," Center for Health and Economy, February 27, 2015.

Tom A. Coburn, MD

CONTINUOUS COVERAGE GUARANTEE

No American wanting to responsibly purchase health insurance should be unfairly treated due to a pre-existing medical condition. Unfortunately, previous efforts to meet this goal have been inadequate. For example, the Health Insurance Portability and Accessibility Act of 1996 promised most Americans the ability to purchase insurance regardless of pre-existing conditions, but the guarantee was only available after consumers met a laundry list of requirements. Even if they followed the right steps—a feat by any estimation—consumers had no assurance their premiums would be anything close to reasonable.

Sadly, the most recent attempt to address this issue, President Obama's health reform law, has actually increased the cost of health insurance. Under the Patient Protection and Affordable Care Act (ACA) the cost of coverage has continued to climb; even with hefty federal subsidies, many Americans with pre-existing conditions still cannot find insurance products with affordable premiums and deductibles.

While the ACA included a ban prohibiting insurers from considering pre-existing conditions when they set individual premiums, it was coupled with draconian, overbearing mandates stipulating that American individuals and employers must purchase insurance or pay fines. Other measures in the ACA, like restrictions on how much older consumers can be charged compared to younger consumers, have already started driving up the cost of coverage for millions of Americans and have limited the formation of innovative plans that are well-suited to what consumers want and need.

Insurers have often had to trim the size of their networks or raise deductibles, leaving consumers with little to choose from besides a handful of bad options. Healthcare spending by the federal government and consumers is ultimately on an unsustainable course, which is why so many of the ACA's provisions should be repealed.

AN ALTERNATIVE TO INEFFECTIVE PROVISIONS OF THE ACA

Our nation needs a way to protect access to health insurance for those with pre-existing conditions *and* empower patients to make the best choices for themselves and their families. The Patient Choice, Affordability, Responsibility, and Empowerment (Patient CARE) Act—a healthcare reform proposed by Senators Richard Burr, Orrin Hatch, and myself in January 2014—would achieve these goals.[1]

To safeguard individuals against being charged more due to pre-existing conditions, the Patient CARE Act would include "continuous coverage" protection for all Americans. Individuals could not be medically underwritten and charged higher premiums, nor could they be denied access to a plan on the basis of a pre-existing condition as long as they have had health insurance for at least 18 months without a significant break in coverage. Protection would apply regardless of which type of plan someone has currently or had previously, whether through a state individual market, an employer, COBRA, Medicaid, or another provider.

A transitional, one-time open enrollment period would allow all Americans to get coverage regardless of prior insurance status and without fear of being medically underwritten. An annual open enrollment period thereafter would give people the opportunity to buy insurance or switch plans.

---

1. Medicare-related provisions of the ACA would be left in place under this proposal, foreseeing the need for broader Medicare reform.

BENEFITS OF THE PATIENT CARE ACT

The Patient CARE Act's continuous coverage provision would reward individuals for purchasing and maintaining insurance but would not impose burdensome and expensive mandates, as the ACA does. While free to choose whatever seems best, individuals would have a strong disincentive to wait to enroll in health insurance until they become sick, lest they be medically underwritten and potentially charged more as a result.

For example, consider the case of Jane, a cancer survivor and mother of a son with severe asthma. She was recently laid off and lost her employer-sponsored health insurance. Under our proposal, she could purchase a new insurance plan on the individual market within 60 days of leaving her previous job, protected by the Patient CARE Act's continuous coverage safeguards. Health insurance companies would be prohibited from charging Jane's family a higher premium based on any pre-existing health conditions. She and her family would essentially be rewarded for their responsible coverage.

If Jane could not afford a new plan, she could still get coverage: targeted tax credits would help eligible families and individuals cover the cost of insurance. The refundable, advanceable credits would be available to individuals and families making up to 300 percent of the poverty level to help them purchase quality health insurance suitable to their needs. These credits would be age adjusted, with older beneficiaries receiving more than younger ones, and also income adjusted.

The Patient CARE Act includes provisions that would help actually lower the cost-drivers of care, putting downward pressure on healthcare costs. People with pre-existing conditions—and all other consumers—would have access to more affordable products than under current law. Eliminating one-size-fits-all mandates would allow insurers to design products that fit the actual needs of consumers rather than following requirements imposed by federal bureaucrats and politically appointed officials.

Access to insurance and protection from unfair denials of coverage or skyrocketing premiums would not be the only benefits of the Patient CARE Act.

States would have the opportunity to use high-risk pools to provide affordable, quality health insurance for high-cost patients. Targeted funding envisioned in the Patient CARE Act could be used to support traditional, single-state pools, or more innovative solutions such as multistate pools that diversify risk regionally. Patients with chronic, costly conditions would benefit from long-term disease management and coordination provided through these pools. And high-risk pools have the potential to reduce premiums across the individual market because costly patients are less likely to be moving among different plans every year—a risk for which insurers otherwise have to account.

Consumers would also gain new tools for comparing and using their insurance. Plans would be subject to strong transparency measures regarding which services are covered and what they cost. These kinds of tools have demonstrated value for consumers, leading to a 13–14 percent reduction in the cost of advanced imaging and laboratory services used by patients, according to recent research published in the *Journal of the American Medical Association*.[2] Other protections included in the Patient CARE Act are prohibitions against lifetime limits and rescissions, except in limited circumstances such as fraud, deliberate misrepresentation, or failure to pay insurance premiums.

CONCLUSION

Our proposal offers a market-oriented path toward making the US healthcare system more competitive, sustainable, and affordable. Moreover, our proposal also respects individual liberty. For example, a 24-year-old in perfect health could make an informed decision to forgo insurance. If he were to later develop high blood pressure and decide to purchase insurance, the insurer would be able to assess his health to determine his risk profile as a beneficiary. His premiums would likely be higher (due to the higher blood pressure) than if he had simply maintained insurance the entire time. This approach protects the most vulnerable, encourages responsibility, and is fair to all Americans.

In the wake of calls to repeal the ACA, anyone with a pre-existing condition (or who may develop one) is right to ask: If I take steps to make responsible choices, will I be denied health coverage at any time because

---

2. Christopher Whaley et al., "Association between Availability of Health Service Prices and Payments for These Services," *Journal of the American Medical Association* 321, no. 16 (2014): 1670–76.

of a medical condition? Will my premiums be fair, or will they be significantly higher than my peers'? Under the safeguards built into the Patient CARE Act, individuals with pre-existing conditions will be protected and all patients will have more freedom and better choices so they can make the best healthcare decisions for their families.

Bradley Herring

GUARANTEED RENEWABILITY AND EQUITABLE TAX TREATMENT

R oughly one-quarter of the nonelderly adult population in the United States has a pre-existing chronic condition. In principle, obtaining private health insurance with an experience-rated premium tailored to a consumer's expected expense for the year would provide a welfare improvement to facing high and uncertain medical spending if uninsured, but society may not like the inequity of those with pre-existing conditions paying premiums as much as 10 times higher than the premiums paid by healthy people. Moreover, even for healthy people, the uncertainty of future increases in one's premium resulting from potentially developing a chronic health condition is something that risk-averse people should want to avoid.

The fundamental hindrance to achieving the goal of pooling comes down to the following policy conundrum: How can policymakers get younger, healthy adults to essentially cross-subsidize older adults with pre-existing chronic conditions? There are ultimately two separate methods policymakers could adopt to tackle this problem: a set of regulation-oriented arrangements that would compel cross subsidies, and a market-oriented arrangement that would establish voluntary cross subsidies.

This market-oriented arrangement of voluntary cross subsidies would be based on guaranteed renewability of insurance and would require a modification of the tax code to extend the tax break for health insurance beyond the employment-based market into the individual market. If that tax inequity were removed, people would obtain guaranteed-renewable insurance while young and healthy, and the pre-existing condition problem would eventually barely exist. This market-oriented arrangement could be superior to the set of regulatory arrangements that have been either tried or suggested to help people with pre-existing conditions.

THE REGULATORY ARRANGEMENTS

The following four regulatory arrangements are widely proposed, or used, in attempts to cross-subsidize people with pre-existing conditions.

The first arrangement is simply a government single-payer model in which everyone has the same amount of coverage financed by government tax revenues. In this situation, there are cross subsidies both from high-income people to low-income people and from people without pre-existing conditions to people with pre-existing conditions. While some view this as the simplest, most elegant arrangement, there are important negative consequences. One is the "deadweight loss of taxation" from lower economic output caused by the higher tax rates needed to finance this coverage. Another is the potential inefficiency from government-administered provider prices, which includes the regulator's costs of determining appropriate prices based on underlying marginal costs and the potential mismatch between prices and marginal costs, owing to either naïve estimates for costs or inappropriate "regulatory capture" of the price-setting system.

The second arrangement is the employer mandate model, in which employers are simply required to offer coverage to workers. Employer mandates set up cross subsidies from low-income people to high-income people (through the regressive tax exclusion for employment-based insurance) and from people without pre-existing conditions to those with pre-existing conditions (because the reductions in worker wages to finance the employer benefit are unlikely to vary by individual health status). In addition to the inequities and inefficiency of the tax exclusion itself, there are also likely important labor market distortions resulting from this mandate on employers. These might include increased unemployment resulting from higher total compensation costs for employers, especially for workers near the minimum wage, where higher benefit costs cannot be offset by lower wages.

The third regulatory arrangement is a community rating provision, making the premiums people pay independent of their pre-existing conditions, coupled with a guaranteed-issue provision, requiring insurers to sell their policies to anyone regardless of pre-existing conditions. The adverse selection by those with chronic conditions essentially needs to be offset by a combination of tax subsidies for the premium and tax penalties for the failure to purchase health insurance. For instance, the state health insurance exchanges set up by the Patient Protection and Affordable Care Act (ACA) couple generous subsidies with an individual mandate's tax penalty. Interestingly, Medicare Part D's prescription drug coverage is essentially community-rated insurance, and similarly mitigates adverse selection by relatively large subsidies and a late enrollment penalty equal to 1 percent of the premium per year.

A final regulatory arrangement couples private experience-rated individual coverage with high-risk pools to provide coverage to uninsurable people who cannot pass medical underwriting to obtain a private plan. This was essentially the arrangement taken by roughly two-thirds of the states before the ACA's passage. Historically, these state high-risk pools were either underfunded or expensive. If pools are underfunded, people with chronic health conditions still pay considerably higher premiums than those without chronic health conditions. And if pools are adequately funded by state governments to provide affordable premiums to enrollees, the negative consequences include (again) the deadweight loss of taxation, as well as potential incentives for those without chronic conditions to forgo obtaining coverage until the need arises. Conceptually, the net financing under the high-risk pool arrangement is similar to the net financing under the community rating arrangement, but these two arrangements differ by whether there is an explicit tax to fund the high-risk pool or there is an implicit tax within the premium paid to cross-subsidize those with chronic health conditions.

A MARKET ARRANGEMENT USING GUARANTEED RENEWABILITY AND EQUAL TAX TREATMENT

There is a market-oriented arrangement that would provide affordable coverage for people with chronic health conditions without disincentivizing people who don't have chronic health conditions from obtaining coverage in a voluntary and private market, and without an individual mandate that forces everyone to obtain coverage. To help illustrate this, return to the fundamental policy conundrum posed above: the challenge of achieving cross-subsidization from people without chronic conditions to people with chronic conditions. As noted above, a year-by-year, experience-rated premium would cause younger, healthy people to face the "risk of becoming high-risk" over a longer time horizon. In this situation, these younger, healthy people would want to insure against the uncertainty of being medically underwritten each year and paying high premiums if they have developed a chronic condition.

Guaranteed renewability in private health insurance markets can achieve this result of having people with and without chronic health conditions pay the same premiums—as long as people obtain insurance coverage before developing their first chronic health condition. How does this work? First, guaranteed-renewable insurance permits consumers to renew their coverage at the same premium, regardless of whether they have developed any new chronic health conditions since obtaining the insurance. Moreover, an "incentive compatible" schedule of premiums over time results in people without chronic health conditions actually purchasing coverage voluntarily rather than avoiding coverage because of adverse selection.

As several economists suggested in the mid-1990s, a guaranteed-renewable health insurance policy can be conceptualized as having two parts to the premium: one part covers the upcoming single year's expected expenses for those without chronic conditions, while the second part covers the cumulative multiyear difference between expected spending with chronic conditions and without them for those who develop their

---

1. Mark V. Pauly, Howard Kunreuther, and Richard Hirth, "Guaranteed Renewability in Insurance," *Journal of Risk and Uncertainty* 10 (1995); John H. Cochrane, "Time-Consistent Health Insurance," *Journal of Political Economy* 103, no. 3 (June 1995).

first chronic condition within the upcoming year.[1] As a result, the "subsidies" to cover the higher costs of people who develop chronic conditions simply come from the voluntarily purchased, long-term components of everyone's premiums.

This long-term structure of premiums is similar to the system used in term life insurance, where insured individuals are protected against increases in premiums resulting from changes in their health status.[2] Estimates of the "front loading" of premiums in the early years to enable lower premiums in later years (necessary to convince healthy older people to stay in the pool instead of exiting) are not so high, and thus an arguably affordable premium path over time can be achieved.[3] While the ratio of underlying spending for 64-year-olds versus 18-year-olds is approximately five to one, incentive-compatible guaranteed renewability ultimately yields a ratio of premiums for 64-year-olds versus 18-year-olds estimated to be approximately three to one—ironically the same level specified for the ACA's modified community rating.

One may ask what prevented a robust individual market with guaranteed renewability from achieving widespread pooling before the ACA. Interestingly, most individual market plans were indeed sold with this guaranteed-renewable provision,[3] but the market was still characterized to a great extent by medical underwriting for new applicants with pre-existing conditions. The inequity of limiting tax subsidies to the employment-based market, coupled with the transitory nature of employment-based coverage as people move from job to job, is likely what led to the large number of middle-aged adults with chronic conditions seeking individual insurance for the first time (after losing their employment-based coverage).

Without this bias in the tax treatment of health insurance, these middle-aged adults with chronic conditions could have simply initiated their subsidized coverage in the individual market when young and healthy and maintained that coverage. Attempting to initiate individual coverage as a middle-aged adult with a chronic condition is problematic

2. Mark V. Pauly, Allison Percy, and Bradley Herring, "Individual versus Job-Based Health Insurance: Weighing the Pros and Cons," *Health Affairs* 18, no. 6 (1999).

3. Bradley Herring and Mark V. Pauly, "Incentive-Compatible Guaranteed Renewable Health Insurance Premiums," *Journal of Health Economics* 25, no. 3 (2006).

because, under guaranteed-renewable coverage, having people with chronic health conditions pay the same premium as people without chronic conditions requires that the former purchased (and maintained) that guaranteed-renewable coverage when healthy.

CONCLUSION

To sum up, providing equitable tax subsidies in an individual market with guaranteed renewability would likely result in a more robust health insurance market that would provide those who develop chronic conditions with continuous coverage at affordable premiums. Guaranteed-renewable insurance allows those with chronic health conditions to pay a pooled premium that is the same as that paid by those without chronic health conditions, but as a result of a voluntary decision to pool together rather than a regulatory requirement to do so.

Moreover, this market-oriented arrangement would not bring about the negative side effects associated with the regulatory arrangements, such as the deadweight loss of taxation, regulatory capture, or higher unemployment. That said, a transition to this market-oriented arrangement would likely have to be coupled with high-risk-pool coverage for those who already have pre-existing conditions, but the need for these high-risk pools would decline over time.

SAFETY, SIMPLICITY, AND TRANSPARENCY

"**W**ell then, what would you do? Just let people die?" Those words were thrown at me the first time I debated a national healthcare program for America, way back in the 1990s. Through all the years since then, I have been hearing some version of them at regular intervals. During the debate over the Patient Protection and Affordable Care Act (ACA), that question was the ultimate resort of anyone arguing in favor of the law: whatever its problems, it was better than letting tens of thousands of Americans die each year.

There are a couple of shaky assumptions underlying the question. The first is that health insurance does a great deal to increase health and reduce mortality. This seems obvious enough, but it's surprisingly hard to tease out of the data.[1] For example, the creation of Medicare, which vastly expanded utilization of health care,[2] seems to have produced no measurable impact on mortality among the elderly in its first 10 years of

---

1. Megan McArdle, "Myth Diagnosis," *Atlantic*, March 2010, http://www.theatlantic.com /magazine/archive/2010/03/myth-diagnosis/307905/; Megan McArdle, "Study: Giving People Government Health Insurance May Not Make Them Any Healthier," *Daily Beast*, May 1, 2013, http://www.thedailybeast.com/articles/2013/05/01/shocker-oregon-health -study-shows-no-significant-health-impacts-from-joining-medicaid.html.

2. Amy Finkelstein, "The Aggregate Effects of Health Insurance: Evidence from the Introduction of Medicare" (NBER Working Paper No. 11619, National Bureau of Economic Research, Cambridge, MA, September 2005).

existence.[3] There is ample evidence that health insurance protects people from financial risk—which isn't surprising, because that's what insurance is for. The evidence that it protects people from premature death is less compelling.

Of course, the financial risk is a real problem—a health-related financial disaster can be devastating for families that go through it. But even if we also assume that there are real, and large, health benefits from providing insurance to people, that still wouldn't mean that the ACA was better than nothing. This is the fallacious syllogism that led America into the Iraq War.

1. Something must be done.

2. This is something.

3. Therefore, this must be done.

And thus we got a bloated, complicated law that still isn't quite working as planned.[4] Fewer people are insured than projected, the insurance is less generous than be expected, the exchanges are in financial trouble, the federal back end to pay insurers still hasn't been built. Worst of all, we've locked in most of the features that people hated about the old system: the lack of transparency, the endless battles with insurers over what is covered and what isn't, the feeling that you are captive to behemoth government and corporate bureaucracies that are more interested in the numbers on their spreadsheets than in what you want out of your health care.

I do think that something should have been done. But not this something. What we should have done is created a system that focused on protecting people from the risk we know they face—catastrophic medical bills—and that sought to preserve the best of the American system rather than the worst—that is, to preserve our endless talent for innovation through markets rather than our decidedly lesser talent for creating and managing massive regulatory bureaucracies.

3. Amy Finkelstein, Robin McKnight, "What Did Medicare Do (and Was It Worth It)?" (NBER Working Paper No. 11609, National Bureau of Economic Research, Cambridge, MA, September 2005).

4. Megan McArdle, "Life under Obamacare," *Bloomberg View*, May 6, 2015, http://www.bloombergview.com/articles/2015-05-06/oregon-shows-how-obamacare-could-remake-insurance-market.

GOVERNMENT AS THE INSURER OF LAST RESORT

How could a government program have freed up markets to innovate? Simple: by getting the government to do something it already does decently well, which is to function as the insurer of last resort. Deposit insurance, pioneered by the United States, has basically halted bank runs. Pension benefit guarantees have made sure seniors don't end up in penury. (The Pension Benefit Guaranty Corporation could be better financed, but that doesn't mean the idea itself is bad.) FEMA essentially functions as an insurer of last resort for people struck by natural disasters. These programs introduce a certain amount of moral hazard, as people take more risks and underinsure themselves in the expectation that the government will pick up the tab. But when you look at the devastation these programs have mitigated, it is hard to call them anything but an overwhelming success.

How would a similar program work for health care? The government would pick up 100 percent of the tab for health care over a certain percentage of adjusted gross income—the number would have to be negotiated through the political process, but I have suggested between 15 and 20 percent. There could be special treatment for people living at or near the poverty line, and for people who have medical bills that exceed the set percentage of their income for five years in a row, so that the poor and people with chronic illness are not disadvantaged by the system.

In exchange, we would get rid of the tax deduction for employer-sponsored health insurance, and all the other government health insurance programs, with the exception of the military's system, which for obvious reasons does need to be run by the government. People would be free to insure the gap if they wanted, and such insurance would be relatively cheap, because the insurers would see their losses strictly limited. Or people could choose to save money in a tax-deductible health savings account to cover the eventual likelihood of a serious medical problem.

ADVANTAGES OF THE INSURER-OF-LAST-RESORT ALTERNATIVE

Of course, anyone proposing an alternative to the ACA, or to the previous status quo, has to be able to say why the alternative is better. In this case, there are three answers to that challenge. First of all, it is dead simple, and the simpler a government program is, the better it works. The ideal government program can be explained to a third grader on a postcard, and this one comes close.

The second reason this is better is that it protects people from actual catastrophic costs better than the existing system, while also being more progressive. Warren Buffett will get nothing out of the system; someone with very little income will have all medical bills paid. No one will have to worry about being slapped with an unpayable bill if, say, an anesthesiologist turns out to be out of network.

But the third and most important reason this alternative is better is that it introduces a key element that has gone missing from health care since third-party payers started to take responsibility for the bills: transparent prices, and consumers who make decisions based on them. Milton Friedman famously divided spending into four categories, which P. J. O'Rourke summarized thus:

1. You spend your money on yourself. You're motivated to get the thing you want most at the best price. This is the way middle-aged men haggle with Porsche dealers.

2. You spend your money on other people. You still want a bargain, but you're less interested in pleasing the recipient of your largesse. This is why children get underwear at Christmas.

3. You spend other people's money on yourself. You get what you want but price no longer matters. The second wives who ride around with the middle-aged men in the Porsches do this kind of spending at Neiman Marcus.

4. You spend other people's money on other people. And in this case, who gives a [damn]?[5]

The first category is what produces market efficiency. Unfortunately, almost no one in the system does that. Instead, we have insurers spending their money on someone else, consumers spending someone else's money on themselves, and the government spending other people's money on someone else. No one gets what he or she wants, vast oceans of times are wasted fighting over what to buy, and it all costs too much.

Of course, some things are too expensive to get price discipline from this system: organ transplants, very early preemies, many forms of cancer. But there's little price discipline in those areas now, so we wouldn't be any worse off. Meanwhile, lots of areas, from hospital beds to the details of knee surgery, would for the first time in decades be subject to the decisions of consumers who care both about getting what they need and about how much they're spending.

CONCLUSION

I spent years uninsured in my twenties, and remarkably, I got the best health care of my life, because doctors stopped performing tests and procedures "just in case" and thought hard about what was necessary. I was obviously taking an enormous financial risk, and the government can usefully mitigate that. But I was also an empowered consumer rather than a number in our vast healthcare bureaucracy. A better future for American health care would be one where more people are uninsured and fewer of them are at risk.

5. P. J. O'Rourke, *Don't Vote: It Just Encourages the Bastards* (New York: Atlantic Monthly Press, 2010), 67–68.

James C. Capretta

EXPLORING SUPERIOR APPROACHES TO THE ACA

Some observers might question the usefulness of ongoing policy discussion about health insurance coverage for pre-existing conditions. After all, as of January 2014, insurers are barred from excluding such conditions from their policies, even for short periods, by the Patient Protection and Affordable Care Act (ACA). Moreover, insurers are no longer allowed to charge higher-than-average premiums to consumers with higher-than-average expected health costs. In short, many would say the ACA has solved the problem, so there's nothing more that needs to be discussed.

There is little reason, however, to presume that the ACA's approach to addressing the issue will work as planned. Implementation of the law's insurance regulations is still in an early stage, with the major changes in effect for less than two years. Moreover, the ACA's reforms closely track previous efforts tried in several states, including Kentucky and Washington, in the 1990s. Those state-led efforts eventually collapsed because premiums soared and insurers fled the marketplace. The problem was one of distorted incentives. Like the ACA, these state laws barred insurers from excluding pre-existing conditions from coverage, required insurers to take all comers, and strictly limited the use of medical underwriting in setting premiums. The healthy responded to the new rules by dropping coverage because they knew they could re-enter the market later with no penalty.

Meanwhile, many consumers with expensive health problems jumped at the chance to buy insurance with strictly regulated premiums. The result was an unbalanced risk pool that could not be sustained.

The ACA is different from these state efforts in one important respect: individuals are ostensibly required under the new federal law to enroll in health coverage—the so-called "individual mandate." The state efforts from the 1990s had no such requirement. The intended effect of the mandate is to prevent the healthy from fleeing the market.

Will it work? It is too early to make a definitive assessment. The Department of the Treasury reports that 6.6 million households paid the tax for going without coverage for some period of time in 2014, and reports indicate that many of them declined to sign up for coverage for 2015 when given the opportunity to do so.[1]

To soften the political blowback from the mandate, the administration announced that individuals can apply for exemptions based on a number of different circumstances, including experiencing any kind of hardship that might make it difficult to pay premiums. The effectiveness of the mandate will depend in large part on whether this exemption process becomes a gaping loophole for evading the tax. It will not be easy for the administration to strictly enforce the individual mandate, which remains one of the most unpopular provisions in the entire law.

AN ALTERNATIVE TO THE INDIVIDUAL MANDATE

It is possible to construct an alternative approach to providing secure insurance for the sick that does not rely on a provision as unpopular as the individual mandate. The foundation for this approach would be a new federal rule: people who stay continuously covered by health insurance would be protected from their health status factoring into the premiums they owe or the coverage they can secure. This new protection would allow consumers to move seamlessly between insurance platforms—employer

1. Area of Focus #3 in Taxpayer Advocate Service, "National Taxpayer Advocate Objectives Report to Congress, Fiscal Year 2016," vol. 1 (Publication 4054, Internal Revenue Service, n.d.); Stephanie Armour, "Many Uninsured Choose Penalty over Enrollment Offer under Health Law," *Wall Street Journal*, March 20, 2015, http://on .wsj.com/19a1JuU.

plans, the individual market, and public insurance—without fear of being penalized financially based on their medical history.

Previous congressional action has already partially built this new protection into insurance law. The 1996 Health Insurance Portability and Accountability Act prohibited employer plans from excluding pre-existing conditions from coverage for newly hired workers and their families so long as the worker had not experienced a lengthy break in coverage. This new protection made it much easier for workers to move between job-based insurance plans.

Unfortunately, the 1996 law's effort to provide similar protection for those moving from job-based insurance to the individual market was flawed. Among other problems, workers lost their right to protection if they did not avail themselves of so-called COBRA coverage from an employer before moving to "individually owned" insurance. Because COBRA coverage is generally quite expensive, most workers who left their jobs never bothered to sign up for it and thus were forced to face medical underwriting when they wanted to buy insurance in the individual market.

A new federal law could put an end to the problem by providing iron-clad "continuous coverage" protection that would allow those who stay insured (with minimal breaks in coverage) to move from job-based coverage to the individual market, and vice versa, without fear of coverage exclusions or higher premiums based on their health status.

CORRECTING THE TAX TREATMENT OF HEALTH INSURANCE

Of course, critics will note that continuous coverage protection is extended only to those *with* insurance, and thus implicitly to those who can afford to pay the premiums. What about low-income households, or the unemployed, who have limited resources? For this approach to work, it is also necessary to address a long-standing inequity in federal tax law. Workers enrolled in employer-sponsored health insurance plans enjoy a generous federal tax break that, before enactment of the ACA, had not been extended to those who must buy insurance on their own. Employer-paid premiums are excluded entirely from both federal income taxes and payroll taxes. By contrast, before 2014, a consumer purchasing insurance directly from an insurer had to pay the premium entirely from after-tax dollars. The ACA provides premium credits to people with incomes above Medicaid eligibility but below 400 percent of the federal poverty line who buy their insurance through the law's exchanges. The law, however, does not provide tax equity for households with higher incomes and without access to an employer plan.

It is possible to develop a comprehensive solution for pre-existing conditions and tax equity that fully replaces both the ACA's regulations and its premium credit subsidies. One option would be to provide households without access to an employer plan with a refundable tax credit of roughly equivalent value to the tax break for job-based insurance.[2] The tax credit could then be used by the unemployed and others who don't have access to employer coverage to stay continuously insured and retain the regulatory protection that being insured would provide.

This tax credit for those outside the employer system could be financed in part by putting an upper limit on the tax break for employer coverage. For instance, employer-paid premiums could be fully excluded from income and payroll taxes owed by a worker, but only up to a limit of about $20,000 for a family plan or $8,000 for an individual policy. Only the most expensive job-based insurance plans have premiums exceeding these thresholds.

Although the tax credit would be available to anyone without access to an employer plan, it is likely that many millions of households would still fail to avail themselves of the credit and thus remain uninsured. That has been the experience with other federal credits and programs, where take-up is far from 100 percent among eligible households. To expand insurance enrollment, and thus also to maximize the number of people retaining continuous coverage protection, the new tax credit for insurance could be coupled with a new, state-administered "default enrollment" option. States would be allowed to assign credit-eligible households that fail to use the credit to a default private insurance product. The insurance companies offering default insurance would adjust the up-front deductibles as neces-

---

2. The health reform plan proposed by Senator Richard Burr, Senator Orrin Hatch, and Representative Fred Upton in January 2015 includes a tax credit of this kind, as does the reform plan sponsored by the 2017 Project (a conservative nonprofit). See 2017 Project, "A Winning Alternative to Obamacare," accessed October 8, 2015, http://2017project .org/2014/01/paving-way-full-repeal/#.VhaG9bRViko.

sary to ensure that the premiums for the plan remain identical to the value of the credits. This would ensure that enrollees get at least catastrophic insurance protection without having to pay any premium themselves. Everyone enrolled in a default insurance plan would retain continuous coverage protection, but there would be no requirement that households accept the default coverage. At any time, they could voluntarily opt out of the insurance plan.

CONCLUSION

The ACA established heavy and extensive new regulations to expand insurance enrollment and "solve" the pre-existing condition problem. The law remains on uncertain political ground, however, in large part because the public remains uneasy about the extensive federal role in, and the related high costs of, the supposed solution. The political door is open, therefore, for the presentation of an alternative approach that solves the problem with far less burdensome federal rules. The approach outlined here is just such an alternative, and should therefore be taken seriously by policymakers who are unsatisfied with the ACA.

Charles Blahous

TOP EXPERTS PRESCRIBE BETTER PATHS FORWARD

The Patient Protection and Affordable Care Act (ACA) attempts to facilitate insurance coverage for those with pre-existing health conditions through the combination of a comprehensive coverage mandate, guaranteed issue, and community rating, among other provisions. The essays in this collection validate the Mercatus Center's solicitation of multiple perspectives, from several leading health policy experts, on the best alternatives to this controversial approach. Where one expert has left a particular angle uncovered, another has likely addressed it. The compilation as a whole presents a variety of worthy approaches, while certain themes recur throughout the collection.

One such theme is the ongoing policy damage caused by the long-standing tax preference for employer-sponsored health insurance. The problems created by this tax distortion are enormous. It has distorted labor markets in favor of employee compensation in the form of healthcare benefits over wages, thereby putting upward pressure on healthcare prices and costs. It has inhibited the development of a robust market serving individual health insurance customers. And as Bradley Herring points out, the tax preference is also regressive, preferentially subsidizing more highly compensated workers. The tax distortion has also undercut market solutions to the pre-existing condition coverage problem, as discussed later in this essay.

ASKING INSURANCE TO DO TOO MUCH

Perhaps the strongest impression left by the accompanying essays is that the ACA's comprehensive insurance mandate is an example of legislative overkill in response to a policy challenge. That challenge is to protect Americans from financial hardship arising from high individual health-care costs. Such high health expenditures might be either temporary or permanent, and they could arise either unpredictably or predictably as a result of a long-term condition. A workable solution must address all these possibilities.

The relevant purpose of insurance here is nevertheless narrow: specifically, to pool risk. Insurance generally exists to protect holders from the possibility of an undesirable event. This risk protection function need not necessarily be mixed with other compelling policy agendas such as broader income support goals and which healthcare services Americans should receive. Indeed, as Megan McArdle notes in her trenchant piece, it is the shoehorning of so many ill-fitting policy agendas into the health insurance system that in large part causes the purchase of healthcare to be as unpleasant as it is for so many Americans. We are simply asking insurance to do too much—more than it is equipped to do.

Most Americans do not want anything so complicated out of their healthcare financing system. They simply want good-quality service at a competitive price, just as they see successfully delivered to them in other markets. In this context they surely need financial protection against healthcare expenses surpassing what they can afford. This objective of protection against financial hardship, however, does not imply the necessity of a mandate to purchase comprehensive health insurance along parameters of government design.

Indeed, despite the initial arguments made on behalf of the ACA's coverage mandate, it has since become clear that neither the ACA's proponents nor its opponents regard the mandate as a necessary feature of national healthcare policy. After all, the ACA's opponents argued against the mandate before the law's enactment, with some challenging its constitutionality afterward all the way to the Supreme Court. The essays in this collection reflect the views of many such experts: that a comprehensive coverage mandate embodies more intrusion into the insurance market than is necessary or desirable to address the policy challenge. The ACA's proponents, meanwhile, have pronounced the law a success despite the fact that the mandate and its accompanying penalties have not generally been enforced. Given these respective behaviors, we are led to the conclusion that neither side in this polarized debate regards the mandate as truly essential to the purpose of protecting those with pre-existing conditions.

PROTECTING THOSE WHO MAINTAIN CONTINUOUS COVERAGE

Many of the essays here, including those of Herring, James Capretta, former Congressional Budget Office director Douglas Holtz-Eakin, and former senator Tom Coburn, advocate that individuals be held harmless from insurance underwriting based on their medical conditions, provided that the individuals meet some standard of previous continuous coverage. Capretta notes that this simple measure would largely "put an end to the problem" without relying on a provision "as unpopular as the individual mandate." Any such continuously covered individual would be protected from having a later health condition factor into the pricing of his or her health insurance. This framework would provide a powerful incentive for individuals to enroll in coverage while their individual health costs are still low, thereby protecting themselves from costs associated with the later development of expensive health conditions.

Herring observes in his essay that individual health insurance products have long included such guaranteed renewability provisions; nevertheless, they were often unavailable to individuals moving from employer-provided insurance, leaving plans featuring medical underwriting to dominate the individual insurance market. The absence to date of a market solution to this problem appears to be another adverse effect of the tax preference for employer-provided health insurance; Herring suggests that the tax distortion has resulted in a "large number of middle-aged adults with chronic conditions seeking individual insurance for the first time."

SUBSIDIZING THOSE IN NEED THROUGH HIGH-RISK POOLS

Holtz-Eakin acknowledges that a continuous coverage system does not by itself overcome the challenges facing "those whose pre-existing conditions currently price them out of the insurance market." And as Coburn notes, any system that preserves liberty will involve some individuals who make "an informed decision to forgo insurance" even if there were powerful monetary incentives to carry it. We thus need a policy that would provide for those who have an expensive health condition when they enter the health insurance market, whether this has resulted from choice or uncontrollable circumstances.

Given that our societal value judgment favors providing support for those facing high healthcare costs, the simple answer, according to Holtz-Eakin, is to subsidize those for whom "the ratio of health costs to [individual] income is too high." McArdle offers a simple and transparent way to accomplish this by doing away with the maze of complicated federal health entitlements and having the government act solely as the "insurer of last resort," picking up the tab for health expenses exceeding a defined share of an individual's income.

Several of the essays endorse high-risk pools as a straightforward approach to insuring individuals with high healthcare costs. This too would have the important virtue of increasing transparency—an attribute too often evaded by political actors, but indispensable to voters and taxpayers attempting to make informed judgments about public policy. A high-risk pool is a mechanism governments can use to subsidize insurance coverage for those with large healthcare bills. Rather than concealing the extent of such support through a complex and opaque system of insurance cross-subsidization that drives up everyone's healthcare costs, high-risk pools would transparently concentrate such subsidy support where Americans agree it is most appropriate. Herring observes that the need for high-risk pools should decline over time the longer that guaranteed renewability is in place.

CONCLUSION

In the end, however, Robert Graboyes's observation bears emphasis: our national discussion about healthcare has been "mired in a furious, partisan debate over how to distribute fixed stocks of resources" which, no matter how it is decided, can never please all the participants. Indeed, the ongoing debates over such particulars as guaranteed issue, community rating, and even the general subject of covering pre-existing conditions are essentially arguments about how to distribute benefits and burdens assuming a fixed supply of healthcare services. Yet Graboyes also observes that today "residents of the humblest villages in the developing world carry phones more powerful than 1980s supercomputers," a distributive achievement paradoxically made possible by prioritizing innovation over distribution. To the extent that national healthcare policies focus narrowly on redistributive questions rather than on improvements in healthcare quality, they will fail to fulfill Americans' healthcare desires. Any decisions we make to protect those facing expensive health conditions must not have the effect of constraining the rate of broader healthcare quality improvements. This may be the best reason of all for replacing an overly prescriptive comprehensive coverage mandate with an alternative approach that fosters the development of a vibrant healthcare market.

ABOUT THE EDITORS

Robert Graboyes is a senior research fellow and healthcare scholar with the Mercatus Center at George Mason University and is the author of the study "Fortress and Frontier in American Health Care." He earned his PhD in economics from Columbia University. An award-winning teacher, Graboyes holds teaching positions at Virginia Commonwealth University and the University of Virginia.

Charles Blahous is a senior research fellow at the Mercatus Center at George Mason University and director of its Spending and Budget Initiative research program. He has also served as a public trustee for Social Security and Medicare. Blahous specializes in domestic economic policy and retirement security with an emphasis on Social Security, as well as federal fiscal policy, entitlements, demographic change, and healthcare reform.

ABOUT THE CONTRIBUTORS

Douglas Holtz-Eakin is president of the American Action Forum policy institute and a former commissioner on the congressionally chartered Financial Crisis Inquiry Commission. He was also formerly director of the nonpartisan Congressional Budget Office and chief economist on the president's Council of Economic Advisers.

Tom A. Coburn served in the US Senate between 2004 and 2014. Before his tenure as one of Oklahoma's senators, he served three terms in the US House of Representatives. While in Congress, Coburn held seats on the Homeland Security and Governmental Affairs Committee and the Senate Judiciary Committee. Coburn is also a licensed medical doctor.

Bradley Herring is associate chair for academic programs, director of the PhD concentration in health economics and policy, and an associate professor at the Johns Hopkins Bloomberg School of Public Health. He has served on the president's Council of Economic Advisers and currently serves as chair of the Board of Directors for the Maryland Health Insurance Plan.

Megan McArdle is a columnist for *Bloomberg View*, where she writes on economics, business, and public policy. She is the author of *The Up Side of Down: Why Failing Well Is the Key to Success* and founder of the blog *Asymmetrical Information*. McArdle has also written for *Newsweek*, the *Daily Beast*, the *Atlantic*, and the *Economist*.

James C. Capretta is a senior fellow at the Ethics and Public Policy Center and a visiting fellow at the Mercatus Center at George Mason University. He was formerly the associate director of the White House's Office of Management and Budget. He has also served as a senior health policy analyst at the US Senate Budget Committee and the US House Committee on Ways and Means.

STEPPI[barcode]

STEPMOMS

STEPPING-STONES
for
STEPMOMS

EVERYDAY STRENGTH
for a BLENDED-FAMILY MOM

KARON PHILLIPS GOODMAN

NEW HOPE
PUBLISHERS

Birmingham, Alabama

New Hope® Publishers
P. O. Box 12065
Birmingham, AL 35202-2065
www.newhopepublishers.com

Library of Congress Cataloging-in-Publication Data

Goodman, Karon Phillips.
  Stepping-stones for stepmoms: everyday strength for a blended-family mom / Karon Phillips Goodman.
    p. cm.
  ISBN-13: 978-1-59669-086-8 (soft cover)
  1. Stepmothers--Religious life. 2. Christian women--Religious life.
I. Title.
BV4529.18.G67 2006
248.8'431--dc22
                              2006026552

All Scripture quotations, unless otherwise indicated, are taken from *The Holy Bible*, King James Version.

Scripture quotations marked (RSV) are taken from the Revised Standard Version of the Bible, copyright 1952 [2nd edition, 1971] by the Division of Christian Education of the National Council of the Churches of Christ in the U.S.A. Used by permission. All rights reserved.

Scripture quotations marked (NIV) are taken from the HOLY BIBLE, NEW INTERNATIONAL VERSION®. NIV®. Copyright©1973, 1978, 1984 by International Bible Society. Used by permission of Zondervan. All rights reserved.

Scripture quotations marked (NKJV) are taken from the New King James Version. Copyright © 1982 by Thomas Nelson, Inc. Used by permission. All rights reserved.

ISBN-10: 1-59669-086-0
ISBN-13: 978-1-59669-086-8

N064145 • 0407 • 5M1

Dedication

*To all the stepmoms everywhere
who need our prayers. May we
support and sustain one another
in God's love and care.*

Contents

Coping

Growing

Acknowledgments

I'm so honored to have been touched by the lives of the many stepmoms who inspired and continue to support this book. The sisterhood of stepmoms who understand each other without a word is an amazingly strong and powerful group. They are truly the Lord's disciples.

I greatly appreciate all of those who gave a part of themselves for this book, including my husband and my boys, even though they'll probably never realize the wonderful gifts they've given me. And, I'm truly honored to have Nicole's foreword and the stories from Paige, Shauna, Sue, Kimberly, and Liza to include for you here.

I want to thank everyone at New Hope Publishers, especially Andrea Mullins and Joyce Dinkins. I'm so grateful for their care and dedication.

Finally, I thank *you*, my reader, for joining me on this journey of prayer. Thank you for opening up yourself to the grace of God and reaching out to those around you to share it.

Foreword

It's quiet. It's early. My coffee is hot. The sky is still black. The world is still asleep. The day is coming.

In a few moments the day will arrive. It will roar down the track with the rising of the sun. The stillness of the dawn will be exchanged for the noise of the day. The calm of the solitude will be replaced by the pounding pace of the human race. The refuge of the early morning will be invaded by decisions to be made and deadlines to be met. For the next 12 hours I will be exposed to the day's demands.

It is now that I should pray for strength . . . but there is so much to do. Before I know it, my mind is caught up in the details of the day . . . emails to attend to, deadlines to chart, checkups to schedule, grocery lists to make, breakfast to cook, and bottles to make. Already, my mind is so far away from Him that I can't possibly find the peace He has planned for me.

As I stumble through my tasks, my conscience starts to get to me. When I remember how Jesus taught us to pray, it's so evident to me that He doesn't necessarily want us to repeat the words. He wants us to grasp the message of loving, living, breathing communication in His example:

> *"Pray then like this: Our Father who art in heaven, hallowed be thy name. Thy kingdom come. Thy will be done, on earth as it is in heaven. Give us this day our daily bread; and forgive us our debts, as we also have forgiven our debtors; and lead us not into temptation, but deliver us from evil"* (Matthew 6:9–13 RSV).

"Our Father who art in heaven, hallowed be thy name." What a poetic way to remind us that our Father, our intimate and loving Father, is in control! What problems could I possibly have that can't be handled by my Father, who is in heaven, whose name is honored and praised by all creation?

"Thy kingdom come." There is no other who can compare to our heavenly Father. He reminds us that we are on a journey, and our ultimate reward lies in the fact that God does rule over all and His kingdom will reign over every trial and hurdle we must face.

"Thy will be done, on earth as it is in heaven." Praying for God's will is a beautiful reminder that God only desires to give us the very best. We shouldn't come to the Father with a shopping list. We should come humbly, seeking His face and His good will in our lives, because—like any loving Father—He wants the best for His children.

"Give us this day our daily bread." We fool ourselves if we think we have anything beautiful and good in our lives as a result of our own strengths and talents. Our talents are gifts God has given us to make our way in this world. The opportunities for knowledge and skill are also from God. In His mercy and grace, He gave them to us. Our needs (not necessarily our wants) will always be taken care of if we simply hand the task over to our loving, caring Father.

"Forgive us our debts, as we also have forgiven our debtors." It is no accident that Jesus included this part in His example of prayer. We should forgive those who caused us pain. We are forgiven of our sins to the same degree that we forgive others. Jesus shows us to release the judgment to God the Father and not seek our own revenge. Harboring resentments and revenge creates a self-made prison by our own choosing. Our Father is a God of reconciliation. He set the example with Jesus who paid the price to set us free. He knew that by releasing those who have sinned against us, that we would live a life blessed and filled with joy and happiness . . . a life ready to receive His blessings. It's impossible to live in peace when barriers of resentment and revenge stand in our way.

"Lead us not into temptation, but deliver us from evil."
If we were never tempted, we would never understand or know the will of God and His power to keep us from all forms of evil. We are only a prayer away, and He wants us to pray to help us overcome temptation and grow in faith and character as a Christian. God has promised that He won't allow us to be tempted beyond what we can bear. (See 1 Corinthians 10:13.) Praying for His help in our daily trials is a loving reminder that nothing is too difficult for Him to guide us through.

God has shown Himself to have a very unique way of speaking to us in our daily lives—burning bushes, apparitions, angels. God does speak to us, and the list of His vessels goes on. Remaining in a state of constant prayer enables our hearts to stay open to Him, so He can speak through even the simplest of means . . . even through our "still, small voice."

So I stop and pray.

"Father God, thank You for Your holiness and Your power over my life, and thank You for calling me back to You through Your truth this morning. I pray for Your loving will to be done in my life today. Use me as a vessel to speak Your truth and continue Your loving care of my family and me as I follow the path You have set before me. Forgive me, Lord, for my sins and my shortcomings. Help me, Lord, to forgive those who let me down, as well. Please help me to remember that the journey is mine, and the judgment is Yours. Help me to remember Your example of love in all of my encounters today. Help me, Lord, to claim Your victory over the temptations I will face today, and help me to be a loving example of Your kindness in all of my exchanges. Thank You for You, and for the me I am striving to be. Amen."

The sun is rising now. My coffee is gone. The birds are singing in the new day. My chaos is gone, and I face today with a smile of peace. God did it again. He conquered my noise with His song.

The path of stepparenting isn't always an easy one. Thankfully, for us, God knows our journey, and He knows our trials. He knows our needs before we even speak them. Finding peace in that power is only a prayer away.

Nicole L. Weyant

Nicole L. Weyant, PhD, is a certified blended-family consultant with the International Stepfamily Foundation and founder of the online blended family support group, iStepfamily.com (http://www.istepfamily.com). She is an active member of the American Association of Christian Counselors and the International Association of Coaches.

Introduction

*But I call to God, and the Lord saves me. Evening, morning
and noon I cry out in distress, and he hears my voice.*
                                        —Psalm 55:16–17 (NIV)

Stepmothering is an ultimate learning experience, full of insights
and discoveries, pain and joy. The role is always surprising and
often exasperating. The realization of all you've gotten yourself
into is sometimes overwhelming. The most important thing a
stepmom learns is the most basic and sometimes the hardest to
admit: *I can't do this alone.*

No one ever enters a remarriage with little plans. That
would be too easy! We always have great ideals and greater
expectations. A life—one we never knew we would live—gets
in the way, and almost everyone, including us, will fall short of
those expectations. Very little happens the way we envision, and
we often deal with thoughts, emotions, and fears that shock and
consume us. The faith we claimed and felt before we became
stepmoms is tested. Sometimes it's broken. The past can depress
us, the present exhaust us, and the future terrify us. We may be
tempted to give up, let the pain win, and abandon our hopes for
happiness. Sadly, many stepmoms do.

As many as two-thirds of all remarriages with children
involved end, often before the fourth anniversary. Before
I became a stepmom, that statistic probably would have surprised me, because I thought that people who remarry must be
truly happy—so thankful to have been given a second chance
at the kind of love everybody wants. How could those couples
ever fail?

Then when I became a stepmom and walked through my
own hell, I was surprised that the percentage was only two-
thirds. I'll bet that many of us have wondered—at least once

in the most private moment—whether we would make it, whether we would ever get through the pain and confusion that threatened our marriages, and even more, our faith. That's when it's time to stop questioning your faith and start relying on it instead. That's when you cry out, "Help me!" and the Lord responds.

> *For I, the Lord your God, will hold your right hand,*
> *saying to you, "Fear not, I will help you."*
> —*Isaiah 41:13 (NKJV)*

In this book, we'll go through four stages of a stepmom's life and faith: beginning, struggling, coping, and growing. While stepmoms are all different, we are all very much the same: We help to raise another woman's children; try to keep a burdened marriage together; and we have to learn how, when, and where we fit in unforseen life situations. This is challenging. But God is able.

May each Scripture, prayer, and stepmom's testimony in this book be a stepping-stone of strength to help guide you as you walk your stepmom path. May this book comfort you, encourage you to listen to God, and bring you, step-by-step, to a joy and peace that you could never imagine.

Beginning

"When you pass through the waters,
   I will be with you;
And through the rivers, they shall not
   overflow you.
When you walk through the fire,
   you shall not be burned,
Nor shall the flame scorch you.
For I am the Lord your God."

—Isaiah 43:2–3 (NKJV)

Beginning (or Beginning Again)
Issues in the
Life of a Stepmom

- *Love*
- *Fear*
- *Doubt*
- *Insecurity*
- *Patience*

Beginning

The stepmom sat in the dark on her living room floor, crying again, as she had cried before. She prayed a nonsensical prayer, needing everything, understanding nothing. She felt lost and alone, afraid and defeated. She was watching her world collapse around her, the new world she had tried so hard to create and protect.

That stepmom was me. Maybe it's you too. It was a long time ago that I felt so hopeless, but the feelings are easily beckoned to the surface. *It should be easier*, I kept telling myself. *Why is this so hard?*

When I could calm down and string two thoughts together, I could find lots of answers to that question—my husband, his kids, mine, their other parents, time, money, jealousy, insecurity deeper than space—everything that touched me each day. My life was so hard because it was the life of a stepmom, a bewildered creature afraid and unprepared for a most treacherous journey.

Understanding the causes of my sadness was helpful and finding ways to deal with the pain mandatory. But there was one step that had to come first, and it was a surprisingly hard stretch of faith, because I thought it meant admitting more failure.

Instead, it meant finding the only beginning to a better life. I had to stop trying to carry the burdens by myself. I had to rediscover God's strength, courage, and peace, and go to the safest place, which was waiting for me. I had to open my eyes and my heart to a power much bigger than I am, ask for guidance, and let God provide it.

Often, I couldn't even form the words to turn my fears and hurts into a logical prayer. God didn't mind. He knew my pain as well as I did. He was there to help. He always is.

CHAPTER ONE

FOCUSING ON YOUR LOVE

"Love is patient, love is kind. It does not envy, it does not boast, it is not proud. It is not rude, it is not self-seeking, it is not easily angered, it keeps no record of wrongs. Love does not delight in evil but rejoices with the truth. It always protects, always trusts, always hopes, always perseveres."
— *1 Corinthians 13:4–7 (NIV)*

*L*ove truly is blind. It hides the obvious and obscures the dangers. Love makes us throw more than caution to the wind. We may throw reason, fear, hurt, and anger away while we feast on the undeniable emotion that consumes us as no other does. The love that envelopes you with your new husband feels strong enough to banish even the biggest stepfamily worries, especially if you've experienced a loveless or neglectful marriage. Love is blind to all that would threaten it, and so are we. At least for a while.

Sooner or later, the reality hits and brings all sorts of challenges with it: There is a family that existed before this one. The daily burdens can outweigh the amazing love we thought we had. When we have to look at those outside forces that become more real every day, we sometimes retreat, afraid that the love we trusted isn't there anymore, afraid that what's *opposing* us is stronger than what's *supporting* us. Has the love you felt mutinied, leaving you to stand alone to fight for your life?

It can feel like it sometimes. As the challenges of your life become more visible and more difficult, your stress increases and it becomes hard to recall the warm and nurturing thoughts and feelings you had for your husband even a short while ago, or to remember what it was like to receive those feelings from him. We can become so burdened, afraid, angry, and overwhelmed that we have more feelings of resentment than love. But the love hasn't changed—it's just masked by the problems that hurt so much. It's not been defeated; it's just waiting for you to put it into battle.

ONE AGAINST THE WORLD

Find comfort in the safety of the love that you and your husband feel for each other, and work to unleash it when the world gets you down. Fight your way through your struggles with a constant grip on the force that brought you two together in the first place. Do what you must to protect and reclaim your love of a lifetime. And then, let *your love* protect *you*.

> *L*OVE IS POWERFUL ENOUGH TO GUIDE YOU EACH STEP OF THE WAY.

You and your husband are one against the world. Your love isn't a fairly tale; it's a living, breathing extension of God's love that will sustain you when you're weak. It's strong when you believe it is, and it will grow even stronger when you give it the chance to shine. Ask the Lord to show you ways to express your love, to accept more love, and to let your love work in all aspects of your life.

When your heart is hurting or your mind is full of worry and you can't think anymore, take all of those thoughts and mentally throw them on the floor. Replace each one with a single happy memory that washes the love you and your husband have all over you like sunshine. Breathe in and feel that love energizing you. Then you can rest for a while and have the strength to think again. It sounds too simple, but it's a strong place to start.

Every happy moment, every tiny action that epitomizes the love you two share—give thanks for them all. Thank God for the true and honest love that you've been blessed with and honor it each day by never taking it for granted. You and your husband can use your love to navigate the jagged shoreline of your lives. Love is powerful enough to guide you each step of the way.

PROTECTIVE LOVE

Love is uniquely qualified to protect you as you begin your step life, and when you are just trying to make it better. Because your love has grown from loss and grief and often in a hostile environment, you will be extremely reluctant to give it up. The more you revere and celebrate that love, the more it insulates you from the pitfalls of your life.

If your stepkids' mom attacks you, you have a shield to stand between you and her, a love that isn't afraid and isn't weak. If your stepkids are difficult, you have a foundation that keeps you going when the going feels impossible.

The love you have is strong and is meant to be used. Call on it and let it do its job.

NURTURED LOVE

Even when you're fending off attacks or fighting battles anew, remember that your love is something to be cherished. It is a true gift, and you increase its value with attention and devotion.

In all of the turmoil going on around you, remember to put nurturing your love at the top of your list. You spend time with God every day because you love Him and need Him. Do the same with your husband, regardless of what else is happening. See that love exemplified is a constant in your lives. None of us can keep up with this job without a daily shower of love!

> *"Let all that you do be done with love."*
>   —*1 Corinthians 16:14 (NKJV)*

LOVE REFLECTED

We know how much we need God's love to handle the role of stepmom. And strangely enough, we get even more when we give it away. Like the loaves and fishes, the more we act and react out of love, the more love the Lord pours into our lives.

Sometimes it's hard to see that, isn't it? That doesn't matter, though, because we learn to see with our hearts, to feel *inside* the conviction of a love-filled life. Don't be afraid to give out more love than you expect to receive. It's not a competition. It is a chosen way to live your life, and adding the role of stepmom just expands it a little.

Nothing changes about God's love, and He always fills us with more than enough to do our job and meet every responsibility we have. You can trust Him in that.

> *"The only thing that counts is faith expressing itself through love."*
>   —*Galatians 5:6 (NIV)*

To Think About _____

Take your time to complete answers to each of the following questions.

What makes you feel loved by your husband? Be sure to tell him about it.

In what ways do you show your husband that you love him every day?

How can you let your love protect you more in your struggles?

What role does God's love play in your life and role as stepmom?

How can you reflect His love every day to your stepfamily?

To God in Prayer

Lord, thank You for the love that my husband and I feel for each other. We are on a difficult mission, we recognize the challenges, and we need You in every way. Please help us to always value our love and to use its power to protect and sustain us. Help us to spread that love to our children and to build upon it a safe and secure home for us all. Amen.

God's Response

If God encouraged you in some specific way, use this space to record His response.

CHAPTER TWO

OVERCOMING FEAR

For God has not given us a spirit of fear, but of power and of love and of a sound mind.

—*2 Timothy 1:7 (NKJV)*

Regardless of how much you prepare for your stepfamily, there is no way to predict the deep fear that can overtake you. It's easy to become afraid of everything, especially failing in this marriage you've worked so hard to have. Or you might be afraid of rejection from your stepkids, or that you'll never love or like them. Maybe you're afraid you've made a mistake—that you won't be able to handle the problems and complications of a burdened marriage and kids you didn't birth. What do you do with that paralyzing kind of fear? There's only one effective response, and it's a faith undaunted.

We sometimes let our fears get bigger than they have to be. We generalize, sensationalize, and dramatize until we can't see around our fears enough to deal with them. They grab us by the heart and keep us from finding any happiness and peace. Even the good moments are hard to enjoy when the fears are so strong. But there is something stronger. It's both practical and spiritual, and it's essential for stepmoms.

OVERCOMING FEAR WITH FAITH

Faith is the only thing big enough to counteract the fear. But it's not a vague or faraway faith. It's one that you can hold onto today, right now, because it's *inside* you. It's a faith from God who will never let you down. It is a deep belief that you will find a way to cope with everything and survive what's happening to you when you go to Him in complete confidence that He will respond to your pain.

> *He got up, rebuked the wind and said to the waves,*
> *"Quiet! Be still!" Then the wind died down and it*
> *was completely calm. He said to his disciples,*
> *"Why are you so afraid? Do you still have no faith?"*
> —Mark 4:39–40 (NIV)

He can quiet the waves in your life, too, those now and those to come. No, you don't know everything that will happen within your family. You don't know how your marriage will be tested or how your relationship with your stepchildren will grow, but that's OK. You can face all of that without fear if you choose to go on, to put one foot in front of the other, one day at a time, and if you have faith in God to help you through. He never said this would be easy, but He did say that He would never abandon you in this or any other difficulty.

> *I sought the Lord, and He heard me, And delivered me*
> *from all my fears.*
> —Psalm 34:4 (NKJV)

Trust that God will help you through whatever happens, and then put your energies into finding better approaches and solutions instead of worrying about failing. You'll be able to handle whatever happens if you talk to God first—and have faith that He will hear you.

PRACTICAL FAITH

If you let fear set up shop in your heart, then you can't do the things that will help you see how powerless the fear really is. That's the practical part. With just a little faith, you can make a choice that pushes away fear. When you look at a problem as just an obstacle and not an insurmountable issue, you can find a solution. When you see the problem or fear as just one bump in your family's road, then you can see beyond it.

That takes faith, but don't you see? It's the *practical* faith that says, "OK, trust in yourself, your husband, and God. Pray for guidance, listen, and do one thing today to help yourself get over the fear and rejoice in what you've learned."

Fight the fear each day so that you don't let it get bigger than you are. By taking an active, practical step in the direction *opposite* your fear, you move a step closer to God. If your fear says you're going to be unloved by your stepkids, your faith says follow God's guidance and love them first. Do whatever is more about Him and less about the fear. He won't leave you alone.

> *Y*OU CAN MEET AND DEFEAT YOUR FEARS WITH A SINCERE ACT OF FAITH.

SPIRITED FAITH

Of course, you've heard that most of the things we fear never come to pass anyway. That's little comfort if you're living a threatened marriage or a stepmom/stepchild relationship that seems to thrive on hate. Then it's hard to dismiss that fear with a seemingly nonchalant thought. But *spirited* faith is more than that.

Having faith in God's ability to handle everything and trusting Him to help *you* handle everything makes taking those practical steps easier. You can meet and defeat your fears with a sincere act of faith. You don't have to *will* the fears away. You can take steps each day to *send* fears away, leaning on God who is stronger than anything this life brings. There is no problem bigger than He.

> *There is no fear in love; but perfect love casts out fear.*
> —*1 John 4:18 (NKJV)*

For example, set aside a time to explain to your husband what's scaring you; then come up with a plan together, and reinforce your commitment to each other. This action pushes the fear to the back of your mind; a calming faith in the life you've chosen takes center stage; and your marriage grows stronger too. That tiny tiptoe of faith builds on itself, and the fear can't get a decent footing. Soon, you've defeated the fear that threatened your peace.

STEADY FAITH

If you are afraid that you will never have the relationship you want with your stepkids, realize that your faith can outlast the fear if you let it. Walk slowly in faith to work in even the tiniest ways to build the relationship you want. Take one crisis at a time, implementing one practical idea at a time, responding to your stepchild's actions one response at a time. Build on what's good and reject what's bad. Have faith that you will build as much as your stepchild will let you because you can choose to build while you wait—not fear that you won't.

You don't have to fear something that can always improve over time. If you are too afraid to move, you'll miss the opportunities that do present themselves and overlook the slightest bit of progress. Your fears about being a stepmom are groundless when countered with a true and steady faith in God. He knows, though, how scared we get and how lost we feel. That's why He is never farther away than a prayer, why He is always exactly where we need Him.

The Lord is my light and my salvation; whom shall I fear? The Lord is the strength of my life; of whom shall I be afraid?

— *Psalm 27:1 (NKJV)*

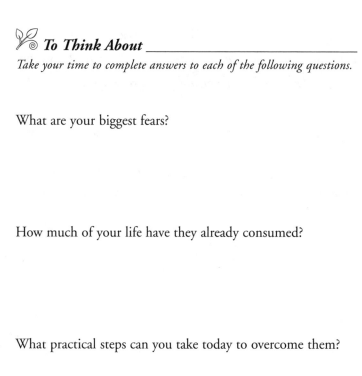

To Think About _____

Take your time to complete answers to each of the following questions.

What are your biggest fears?

How much of your life have they already consumed?

What practical steps can you take today to overcome them?

How can you reinforce and call upon your faith to get you through your fears?

To God in Prayer

Lord, You know these fears that paralyze me sometimes. I need to take care of myself and my family and not be afraid of that which I cannot control. Please help me to replace worry with action, listen to Your guidance, and find a way to banish these fears that are standing in the way of my happiness. I don't want to be afraid anymore. Amen.

God's Response

If God encouraged you in some specific way, use this space to record His response.

CHAPTER THREE

DEFEATING DOUBT

If any of you lacks wisdom, he should ask God, who gives generously to all without finding fault, and it will be given to him. But when he asks, he must believe and not doubt, because he who doubts is like a wave of the sea, blown and tossed by the wind.

—James 1:5–6 (NIV)

*F*ew things can destroy your confidence and make you question your future like becoming a stepmom. Every day brings a new problem that you never thought you'd be thinking about. How could you have prepared, and now, how can you respond to everything that's going on around you? When you need a strong heart and belief in your abilities, that's exactly when you can't feel them. And where is God to help you with all this? How can you deal with the doubt that's overtaking your every thought?

You may have been surprised at how quickly your confidence has eroded—in everything. And it's particularly unsettling when you begin to doubt God, when you feel so lost and alone that you wonder if perhaps you've been abandoned. Where is the help and comfort that you're needing now?

Where is the hope and promise that you began this life with? Your faith in your husband may be tested; your patience with your stepkids may vanish; and your decision to marry may look like less than a great idea. The troubling doubts that creep into every thought can derail you quickly from your path. Knowing where the doubts come from is part of the answer. Choosing to defeat them is the other part.

DOUBTS UNDERSTOOD

Whether the doubts are about your feelings for your life now, your abilities, or your worries about God's presence in your life, the answer is the same: restore your confidence and the doubts go away. Restoring your confidence won't be quick, but you can take it one step at a time and build on your successes. Every time you replace a doubt with a truth, you push every other doubt farther away.

Let's look at your doubts about your feelings first. It's easy to be overwhelmed with anger, worry, and sadness—even to the point of feeling only negative emotions. That's when you can start doubting the very basis of your life now—your love and devotion to your husband. If you're not careful, the anger, worry, and sadness will win. You have to have something stronger to beat them.

Go to the source of your pain and see if you can identify exactly what is creating the doubt in your mind. Is it a nagging feeling, a single episode, that's bothering you? Has someone said or done something to make you question your own feelings? Look deep into your doubt. Write down in one sentence what it is and why you feel that way. For example: *I wonder if I've made a mistake with this marriage because I've given up so much and receive so little in return.*

DOUBTS DEFEATED

Then you can choose to defeat that doubt with a truth—respond with a force that can beat it. Find something just as powerful right away and do it:

- Have some alone time with your husband.

- Write about an especially comforting time.

- Plan a family outing.

- Take a break so that you can recharge and get a better perspective on things—anything positive that reconnects you with your true heart.

- Resolve to put your doubt away for at least 24 hours and look for only reaffirming truths during that time. I know that you can find at least one truth that will give a boost to your confidence in yourself and your choices.

Do you doubt your ability to handle the life of a stepmom? Please don't. You can manage this role just as you do all your other roles: with God's help and a clear plan. Again, write down your most prevalent doubts. Maybe you doubt that you'll ever love your stepchildren, that they'll ever accept you, and that you'll ever bond with them given their mom's opinion of you. All of that baggage is real, but it's not more powerful than your strength and desire to be the stepmom you want to be.

Trust yourself to learn this role; ask God to direct you; and do one positive thing today that restores a little confidence, even if it's as simple as having a calm conversation with your stepdaughter or stepson. One step at a time is enough.

Today, I will:

THE MORE DAMAGING DOUBT

Now let's look at your doubts about finding God in your pain. Do you feel that He has forsaken you to deal with this mess yourself? That's easy to do, especially in the raw worry of a new stepfamily. Write that down too. For example, *I don't know where God is now that I need Him so. Why doesn't He answer my prayers?*

Then choose to defeat that painful doubt with a truth. When has He ever abandoned you? When has He not given you the wisdom, courage, or strength that you needed when you asked Him sincerely? When has He ever been unfaithful to you? How strong is your side of this argument?

> *T*RUST HIM,
> AND YOU
> LEARN
> TO TRUST
> YOURSELF
> EVEN MORE.

Now is just another part of your journey. The scenery changes, but the Guide is the same. God is there with you always, because He can't be anywhere else. Trust Him, and you learn to trust yourself even more.

> *I will say of the Lord, "He is my refuge and my fortress, my God, in whom I trust."*
>
> —*Psalm 91:2 (NIV)*

 *To Think About* _____

Take your time to complete answers to each of the following questions.

What are your most frightening doubts, about yourself, others, or God?

Why have you let them into your heart?

How much are they controlling your life?

Ask God to help you defeat your doubts, find the truths you need to exile them from your heart, and feel a renewed devotion to your family.

To God in Prayer

Lord, please remove all of these hurtful doubts from my heart. I need to feel You close and strong, eager to help me overcome all these questions in my mind. Please speak Your timeless truths to my spirit and guide me confidently through my role as stepmom and wife. Amen.

God's Response

If God encouraged you in some specific way, use this space to record His response.

Chapter Four

Replacing Insecurity with Trust

He will not let your foot slip—he who watches over you will not slumber.

—*Psalm 121:3 (NIV)*

Perhaps the feeling more widespread than any other among stepmoms, new or otherwise, is that of intense insecurity. Sometimes, that insecurity can last for months or even years, depending on how many things threaten our sense of calm and trust. Possibly the insecurity will last only through the first awkward months of establishing a new family. But sometimes, there are tensions and dangers that make settling in a very slow process.

Often the insecurity is a heavy, pervasive feeling of not knowing where you belong. If you've come from a difficult marriage or been abandoned, you may have a hard time trusting your new relationship, especially when it's saddled with the added complications of a husband's former wife and their children. Sometimes, stepmoms talk about feeling "on the outside looking in" at what is supposed to be their new life. They speak of a bond that their husbands have with their kids, a sacred circle that's not easily entered.

Other stepmoms feel that they compete with their stepchildren's mom, for the kids' affection, respect, love, everything. Often, stepmoms are more "mother" to their stepkids than the kids' biological mom, but still, they can feel second-best all the time, wondering if they'll ever be appreciated and feel secure in the pivotal, yet often neglected, role they play in the family.

Perhaps one of the worst feelings of insecurity arises from sharing your life with your husband's former wife. You may feel that your life exists at her mercy; that she can and will control what happens to your family. That's a debilitating kind of insecurity that will destroy you from deep inside if you don't overcome it.

THE LORD'S SECURITY, YOUR SECURITY

All of the logic in the world won't help defy the insecurities you feel. You can dispel them in your mind, and they still will ache in your heart—until you fill it with something else. Let the security of God's love and grace into your whole soul, and rest in the safe place He always has for you.

> *Be merciful to me, O God, be merciful to me! For my soul trusts in You; and in the shadow of Your wings I will make my refuge, until these calamities have passed by.*
> —*Psalm 57:1 (NKJV)*

The Lord's protective arms are always around you, to comfort you and help you see everything more objectively. You can trust that He will help you feel more secure every day, and there are two seemingly contradictory ways to do that: look at each threat and look far ahead.

LOOKING NOW

Take a few moments to look at your life as you begin each day. I know that's a great deal of what you find yourself doing, but on this day, identify and define anything specific that you expect to threaten your security today. Then, before those events even happen, counter each with a warm and safe memory that will let you take a breath and rest for a moment. Then you can prepare.

Always talk to your husband and let him reassure you, because it's possible that he might see some things more objectively than you do. Practice applying reason to your insecurities: your world will not end even if something *does* threaten you today. You will find a way through it because you have in the past. Take time to look at all of the things you have overcome, and find strength in your victories. Pray for continued guidance from the Savior, and let yourself rest in the comfort of His security, the security that will never falter.

> *Jesus Christ is the same yesterday, today, and forever.*
> —*Hebrews 13:8 (NKJV)*

If you let the general ever-growing paranoia of insecurity envelop you, it will. But insecurity loses its punch when you dissect it. Again, just the logic of combating your insecurities won't be enough, but it's a good start. Plan exactly how you'll respond to whatever threatens you—what you'll say or the choice you'll make. You can beat the insecurities by *preparing* for them. Trust God to never leave you alone to face the situations that upset you. God's power is so much greater than anything your life can present. He'll give you each day's required amount of strength and energy, if you'll just ask.

*A*NTICIPATE YOUR HAPPINESS IN A FUTURE YOU AND GOD WILL CREATE.

Looking Ahead

Just as important as looking at each situation that threatens you, look at your whole life and where you want to be 5, 10, 20 years from now. Getting there will take all of your best work, and you can't give your best if nagging insecurities are wearing you down. Look beyond those insecurities to a time when you have mastered them all, when you have overcome every threat to your happiness. Look for good things to happen in your life, and anticipate your happiness in a future you and God will create.

The Lord wants you to be fulfilled in your life, to be safe and secure so that you can give to others the same things: a sense of hope and faith and firsthand knowledge of victory in overcoming the odds of a challenging life. So take a moment each day to look far ahead, perhaps to a time when the kids are grown and happy and you and your husband can reap the rewards of all your hard work.

Then when you guarantee yourself the life you want in the future, you have a better attitude about the insecurities that plague you today, granting yourself the power to dislodge them. Trust in God to lead you through the difficult and scary times with strength and blessings you can't even imagine right now, and look positively to a long time from now, when you'll wonder why you ever let the insecurities you feel today bother you for one second.

SECURITY IN THE LORD

A stepmom's life may never be completely free of insecurities, but it can get better every day. And consider this: many lifestyles lead to insecurities—it's all about learning to manage them and always returning to the Lord for the strength, courage, and will to go on. That's security in the greatest power of all.

> *"I can do all things through Christ who strengthens me."*
> *—Philippians 4:13 (NKJV)*

To Think About _____

Take your time to complete answers to each of the following questions.

What causes you the most insecurity in your role as stepmom?

Why have you allowed these issues to take control of your heart and paralyze your work and progress?

What would give you more security?

Ask God to help you find the security you need for your life, and trust Him to walk the path with you.

To God in Prayer

L ord, this insecurity I feel is killing me inside. Please help me find in You and myself the power to carry on and overcome all the threats I fear, real or imagined. Show me the truths and securities of my life that I have trouble seeing. Please guide me through today; make me stronger and more secure; and then guide me through tomorrow. Amen.

God's Response

If God encouraged you in some specific way, use this space to record His response.

CHAPTER FIVE

PRAYING FOR PATIENCE

Wait for the Lord; be strong and take heart and wait for the Lord.

—*Psalm 27:14 (NIV)*

While we're losing our sanity in this new and compli-cated life, we're usually losing our patience too. Our frustration grows daily when things seem to be at a standstill; no one's cooperating; the "blending" isn't happening; and getting settled into a "normal" life sounds like pure science fiction.

It's an understandable reaction: we want everything to be right and good, and we want it *now*! We want stepchildren to be accepting, former spouses to be stable, and our confusion and anxiety to vanish overnight.

Sadly, we can't have all of that, or at least not as quickly as we wish we could. The dynamics of a stepfamily may stretch realization of those ideals to six, eight, even ten years or more. But no matter how long it takes for us to adapt to our role, the Lord will not abandon us in our journey.

He who began a good work in you will carry it on to completion until the day of Christ Jesus.

—*Philippians 1:6 (NIV)*

WHY PATIENCE IS SCARCE

A new stepmom is anxious for her family to "work," to have a safe, warm place that nurtures everyone, protects everyone, and meets her expectations of happiness. Well, that's a lot to put on a new creation! We often fail to realize just how much we're asking our new union to do, and how little time we give it to perform.

> YOU CAN TOLERATE YOUR IMPATIENCE WHEN YOU TEMPER IT WITH PURPOSE.

Even in the best of situations, love, acceptance, understanding, and real closeness between new family members takes a long time. We know that logically, but we're still impatient to get through the tough times and get on to the happily-ever-after times.

We equate any delay or interruption in our timeline to a defeat, but it's not. Slow progress is still progress. It's just the nature of a very slowly developing entity, a stepfamily. It's not a problem until we make it one.

ACCEPTING OUR LIMITATIONS

Becoming a stepmom always means giving up some control. There is no way that you can control everything the way you did before this marriage. There is no way that you can impose your will, timing, or anything else onto everyone in your home. But there is much you can do *within* the limitations of your role. You can tolerate your impatience when you temper it with purpose.

> *To everything there is a season, a time for every purpose under heaven.*
>
> —*Ecclesiastes 3:1 (NKJV)*

Within your impatience, God will speak to you and teach you what you've missed before. While you are still, you can learn. While you are waiting, you can grow.

Use the time to talk to God in a way you never have before. Let Him help you accept your limitations and work within the bounty of what remains. You can learn plenty about yourself, your family, your God—when you stop fighting the battle to control everyone else and surrender to the pace of your life. It's not a loss or a defeat, but a *strategy* instead.

Beginning your stepfamily is a time to learn who you are again and what your role will be. Stop trying so hard to mold and mend, and instead, let the Lord wrap you in His arms and show you the great purposes He has for you. Let Him prepare you for what is to come. The early days (or years) of a stepfamily can make you feel as if you're getting nowhere, but if you use them wisely, you will find amazing benefits.

> *Yet the Lord longs to be gracious to you; he rises to show you compassion. For the LORD is a God of justice. Blessed are all who wait for him!*
>
> —Isaiah 30:18 (NIV)

Pay attention to the purposes before you, and you'll alienate your impatience and put your worries into perspective.

FOCUS ON NOW

I know that focusing on just today is hard to do, especially when *now* is so troublesome. If you and your stepkids can't get along, it's hard to look at that relationship and be patient for better times. But that's part of learning your role and opening yourself up to what God has in store for you.

If you just wring your hands and wait blindly for improvements, or stomp your foot and curse the facts, nothing good will ever come. Use your time to work on what hurts now by taking one step toward where you want to be. You don't have to seek perfection immediately, but you can honor God's purpose for your time when you use it wisely, when you stop focusing on *deadlines* and start focusing on *lifelines*. You'll be surprised how you benefit from this unselfish choice.

A *lifeline* is an extension of God's power through you, and it has two goals. It helps you meet your purpose for your waiting time, and it helps the situation you're impatient with because It's always a positive action.

In keeping with our original example, if your stepchild is not your favorite person right now and the feeling is mutual, you want to develop a good relationship quickly. But your impatience for that runs headlong into your stepchild's resistance, maybe even your own feelings of insecurity. What do you do? Extend a lifeline.

Maybe it's a truce if your stepchild is old enough to understand the concept of starting over. Or maybe it's an invitation into your life that makes you vulnerable before your stepchild, even if you consider that a risk. Maybe it's a plan to focus on only good qualities of your stepchild while giving yourself permission to accept him as he is.

No matter what the situation you're impatient with, a lifeline or two, instead of a deadline, will help. When you say, "I'm working on the relationship with my stepchild, and I can wait for more progress," instead of "We should be the world's most well-adjusted stepmom/stepchild duo by now," you remove your impatience and replace it with purpose. You'll draw a calmer breath and sleep a more peaceful rest when you focus on your progress instead of your impatience. You can bet God's doing the same thing.

Focus on God

The Lord isn't worried about a deadline because His view encompasses everything, past, present, and future. He will grant us the same calm if we will accept it. When we focus on His timing, we are far less concerned with our own. When we're working every day on what we *can* control, build, reach, and hold, we're too busy to waste time being impatient with what we can't. God's timing will prevail. Our job is to prepare ourselves for it.

GOD'S TIMING WILL PREVAIL.

When we look at our slowly unfolding lives that way, we can at least appreciate, if not understand, God's control of the clock. When we do everything we can with our own time, especially listening to God, we can overcome our fitful impatience with faithful action.

The most faithful action is a worship that says God will meet my worries, always, on time, just as I need. We can stop trying to hurry everything along, and instead, meet wholly what each day brings, impatient only to learn and grow in our role. If we can do something every day that brings us closer to God and benefits our family in even incremental ways, then we've done enough. Tomorrow will be here soon enough to do it again.

Show me Your ways, O LORD; teach me Your paths. Lead me in Your truth and teach me, for You are the God of my salvation; on You I wait all the day.
                                        —*Psalm 25:4–5 (NKJV)*

🌱 *To Think About* _____

Take your time to complete answers to each of the following questions.

Where is your patience wearing thin in your family?

How have you squandered time and missed opportunities by being impatient with yourself and others?

How can you give your impatience over to God today and let Him control and guide your work and timing?

What do you imagine might be the benefits of releasing your impatience to God?

Do you need to assure any family member that you will be more patient with them in the future?

To God in Prayer

Lord, You know my impatient heart. Please help me to go to You first with my frustrations and worries and accept Your timing in my life. Please help me use every moment You've given me to grow closer to You. Help me to cherish our walk and trust You to be right on time in all of my stepmothering work. Amen.

God's Response

If God encouraged you in some specific way, use this space to record His response.

A Stepmom Prays . . .

One day in prayer, I questioned God as to His knowledge of a blended family. Can you imagine questioning God's knowledge? It sounds so disrespectful, but God has a way of extending His grace abundantly to our lives over and over again.

I had been feeling defeated as a "step" mother to my new children. God's Word always had the answer to my questions, but I could not find the answer to this one.

I sat quietly, listening for that voice that comes from deep within the soul and ministers to the heart. Then I heard, *"My Son was a stepchild, and part of a blended family."*

That statement startled me. I reread the story in Matthew 1 about Jesus's conception, Joseph and Mary's quiet marriage, and Jesus's birth. How many times I had read this passage, yet never seen that Joseph was Jesus's stepfather. What an awesome task God had given to Joseph, a simple carpenter—to raise the Son of God. The very breath of God was in their family! He was giving me an awesome task too.

My prayer: *God, breathe the breath of Your spirit into my life and family. Joseph learned through his humility that he could become an excellent father to Your Son. I want to be an excellent mother to these children that You have put into my life. You know me better than I know myself, yet You trust me, in all my weakness, with these precious lives. I sit at Your cross, waiting and listening for Your instruction. Teach me Your ways. Amen.*

—**Paige Becnel**, mother of two, stepmom of three

Peace in Beginning

Sometimes you wonder if you're going to make it, if anyone sees how hard you're trying and knows that despite your mistakes, you're doing your best. Children are masters at giving us the encouragement to begin again, time after time.

I always helped my stepsons make small gifts for their mom for Mother's Day. Never anything expensive or elaborate; we'd just have some fun together cobbling a craft they could proudly give to her. One year, it was modeling clay. They molded their creations, we baked them the allotted time, and they painted bright colors they thought Mom would like. After we were done, one of my stepsons asked for the leftover clay and disappeared into his room. He returned quickly, carefully cradling a rather friendly looking dinosaur boasting an *I* followed by a heart and then a *u* scrawled on his belly. "Ooh," I said, "let's get this baked. Mom's really going to like that." He looked right at me. "I didn't make it for Mom. I made it for you." My beautiful, smiling clay dinosaur leans against my bulletin board at my desk now, helping me begin again, whenever I think I can't.

Struggling

"Behold, I am the Lord, the God of
all flesh.
Is there anything too hard for Me?"

—Isaiah 43:2–3 (NKJV)

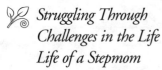 *Struggling Through*
Challenges in the Life
Life of a Stepmom

- *Anger*
- *Resentment*
- *Responsibility*
- *Despair*
- *Envy*

Struggling

Struggling with all the relationships, demands, and feelings of her life may be new for a stepmom, but it's something she gets accustomed to quite quickly. It's amazing how challenging it can be just to bring together two people who love each other. It should be easier, but when those two people bring kids and former spouses and troubles of their own to the mix, the test begins.

Many of us (including me) have wondered whether our family could survive the most difficult times of transition, from two to one, from yours and mine to ours. We wonder if our prayers will be answered, and if we'll truly be able to build something good from so much pain and uncertainty. We wonder how we'll get over the mountain of difficulties in front of us.

God, forever wise, answers: "One step at a time, with Me." With His guidance and constant attention, we can begin to believe that stepmotherhood is something we can manage, even when we struggle daily, still trying to reconcile such unexpected feelings, when we have more questions than answers.

I know the fear and lack of confidence, the thoughts when you look at everything so hard and don't know what to do first. God says to *believe* first, in Him, in the future, in our ability to make sense of our world. He says to kick through the struggles and learn from them, to be better wives and stepmoms as we tame all that would try to rule us.

He says we can do that because He will do it with us. And He can do anything.

CHAPTER SIX

Dealing with Anger

He who is slow to anger is better than the mighty, and he who rules his spirit than he who takes a city.
—*Proverbs 16:32 (NKJV)*

It's not uncommon to hear a stepmom scream in exasperation, "I've *never* been so angry in all my life!" And there are plenty of reasons to get mad—at your husband, the kids, and everybody else in your expanded family. When the anger hits, it can feel like an avalanche on your chest. It's hard to breathe, and as hard as you struggle, you can't move it. It can come quickly, or it can breed over time.

For many stepmoms, confronting one particular kind of anger is a monumental task. They are so angry at the husband's former wife that they can barely function. They are completely consumed by the intense, burning ball of anger that seethes beneath their skin. They are in pain.

Sometimes, it's the comments she makes or the way she twists the truth. Sometimes, it's the way she neglects the kids or unfairly treats their dad. Sometimes, it's her influence on the kids in a way that interferes with the stepmom building a relationship with them. Sometimes, it's her efforts to sabotage and control the stepmom's life. It all hurts, and escaping the anger seems impossible. But it's not.

CORRALLING THE ANGER

When we're angry at someone, there's often just as much hurt as there is anger. We may be hurt and angry because of a direct,

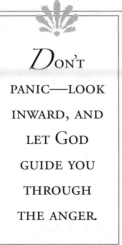

*D*ON'T PANIC—LOOK INWARD, AND LET GOD GUIDE YOU THROUGH THE ANGER.

personalized attack on us or because of someone's actions that are unfair and hurtful to others. We feel pain, disappointment, frustration, and often, the complete inability to do anything about it. Don't panic—look inward, and let God guide you through the anger.

Take a deep breath and tell yourself that you can control and manage your anger. Don't be angry with yourself because you feel angry at the circumstances in your life. These issues are tough to deal with. And, although God understands your feelings, you'll have to make a choice about what to do with your anger. There are only two options: something positive or something negative.

A POSITIVE APPROACH

If you take the negative route, you're likely to lash out at those you love the most, say things you don't mean, and end up with a bigger problem instead of a solution. Do you remember a time when your anger turned you into a monster? The Bible warns us against this kind of response. "Do not be quickly provoked in your spirit, for anger resides in the lap of fools" (Ecclesiastes 7:9 NIV).

A more positive approach is to understand your anger, being sure that you know why you're angry. I know it sounds basic, but your anger is sometimes misplaced or misdirected. For example, you may think you're angry at your husband's former wife because of changes she made with the kids' schedule, but you might really be angry at your husband for allowing it.

When you know why you're angry, then you can make a better choice about what to do about it.

In the example above, discuss your true feelings with your husband, and be sure that he understands your reasoning. Maybe together you two can come up with a plan for the next time a similar situation presents itself. With a combined effort to see the reason for the conflict, you'll be able to get to a solution and not waste your time focusing on your stepkids' mom (whom you can't control anyway).

With a negative approach, you might take your frustration out on the kids, say something you'll regret to their mom, or scar your heart by harboring your hurt and plotting revenge. None of that has anything to do with making peace with your anger.

The Lord's Approach

God's approach is always about resolution. He accepts us when we fail, guides us when we're lost, and shows us how to find what we need when we need it. And He always has an answer for our anger.

It's never about revenge, but *redirection* instead. It's about choosing a positive action for yourself and looking for better uses of your time and talents than retribution.

When you identify and redirect the hostility you feel in a way that works for you, you don't have to suffer anymore. The hurt and the anger are replaced by progress. You make things better by using what you have, and that's always anchored in God's example. The people and events that stir your anger may never change, but the more you work around that anger, the less harassed and victimized you'll feel.

In dealing with that especially challenging anger toward your stepkids' mom, you have to keep in mind that she isn't going away. And as long as her maddening actions continue, you'll have to make a choice. Will you let God show you a positive way to deal with her that starts with *you*, or will you let *her* choices steal your joy? It's your call, and when you claim that power, things change.

How about praying for your husband's former wife? Although this may be the last thing you *feel* that you can or want to do, when you surrender your heart along with your hurt and anger to God, He will enable you to pray for her. You can ask God to forgive her for any hurtful act she has done and to help her not to be angry too. Put yourself in her shoes. She may be hurting in ways you do not comprehend. Ask God to help her and bless her.

The more you seek *resolution*, even if it only means changing your approach, the less angry you'll be about everything around you. And the more likely you'll be to find the answers and peace you seek.

> *Therefore confess your sins to each other and pray for each other so that you may be healed. The prayer of a righteous man [or woman] is powerful and effective.*
>
> —*James 5:16 (NIV)*

To Think About _____

Take your time to complete answers to each of the following questions.

How many hours, days, even years, have you lost to unresolved anger?

How can you better manage your anger instead of letting it manage you?

How can you adopt God's approach and let Him guide you to better choices?

What blessings will you find when you replace your anger with action for peace?

To God in Prayer

Lord, please help me get this anger out of my heart. Help me to see beyond it and to be strong enough to find a positive response in every situation. Steer me away from the words and actions that will only make matters worse. Please stay close and guide me as I seek the solutions that will be best for my family. Amen.

God's Response

If God encouraged you in some specific way, use this space to record His response.

CHAPTER SEVEN

FIGHTING HIDDEN RESENTMENT

*Be joyful always; pray continually; give thanks in all
circumstances, for this is God's will for you in Christ Jesus.*
—*1 Thessalonians 5:16–18 (NIV)*

One particularly unsettling emotion that we often have
to deal with is the strong resentment we can feel almost
from day one. It doesn't put us in a very flattering light, and we
know that it's not the "right" way to feel, but we can't help it. We
know it's not the Christian response, and yet, we're filled with it
to the point of clouding all we think and do.

We have to find a way to deal with the resentment, because
it will only destroy us from inside if we don't. All of the people or
situations we're resenting will still be there—winning—and we'll
be the ones who have lost everything we've tried to build because
we couldn't come to terms with our new responsibilities.

Stepmoms can resent a lot of things, but we'll talk about
just a few. You may see yourself in all of these cases or in none
of them. Either way, we all know that we need a clear and giving
heart to have a happy life. Resentment strangles your heart like
a chicken going to slaughter. God doesn't want you to feel that
way. He can help you find the relief you need.

COMMON RESENTMENTS

Being the mom at your house, whether you're the custodial or noncustodial stepmom, very often means taking full or almost full care of the kids. Dad may abandon their care to you, intentionally or not, simply expecting you to do the daily maintenance because you're "the mom." You may or may not want that kind of responsibility. If you don't, or even if you welcome it but dad doesn't appreciate your efforts, the resentment can grow. You can feel taken advantage of and used, and that's not healthy for you or your family.

> *Y*OU DON'T HAVE TO TRY TO HIDE YOUR FEELINGS FROM GOD.

Another area of resentment is money. It's not uncommon for a stepmom's family to suffer while dad pays large amounts of money to his kids' mom. Even if the amount is fair and spent wisely by the mom, it's still easy to resent making your family do without, perhaps even supporting your stepkids more than half the time. You don't want to seem petty or selfish, but sometimes it's hard to deny those feelings.

Sometimes, stepmoms resent the disruption to their lives. Nothing is easy, and it can seem like every day requires more compromise, more bending to please someone else. You can feel like you're at the bottom of everyone's list, and you don't know how to correct it. You can feel abused and irritated at the same time. It's not a fertile ground for growth.

WHERE TO START

The resentment you feel is both a practical problem and an emotional problem. Tackle it with an application of practical and emotional responses. Get in touch with your spirit so that you can find the strength to get past this stumbling block in your life.

Start with prayer. You don't have to try to hide your feelings from God. You may have felt as I have at times, ashamed of your resentment and yet unable to uproot it. Resentment can be so strong, and it can grow every day. Go to the Lord with your feelings and ask Him to help you understand them so that you can change them. Ask Him to help you see things from His perspective, not just your wounded view. Even if you think He doesn't understand, He does. Asking for His help is the first step in receiving it. Do that today.

Talk to your husband. It may seem an obvious suggestion, but we're often reluctant to discuss such touchy subjects. You may feel that your resentment will come across to him as dissatisfaction or unhappiness, or that he won't understand at all. It's quite possible that your husband doesn't even realize what you're going through. He may have no grasp of your feelings of resentment, your fatigue, your exasperation at everything your life is handing you. So tell him, gently, carefully. Don't make him guess, and don't be afraid to be honest about what's bothering you. You can't build a strong relationship on a foundation of resentment.

Work to make things better at home. As you and your husband discuss these issues, always look for ways to deal with them, and that's what you'll find. When you're specific about the behaviors or circumstances that bother you, then you can be specific about ways to improve them. Ask for the real changes that you need to help alleviate the resentment. When your days improve, even just a little bit at a time, you will feel the resentment drain away from your heart. Actively involve the kids as well. Let them know that there is a new way of doing things. And then don't be afraid to revisit the issue again if things don't get better and stay better.

Count your blessings. I know it sounds trite, but it's hard to feel resentful and thankful at the same time. Consciously look for positive experiences in every part of your life. Look for ways that others are considerate and thoughtful of you, and cherish those moments. Give thanks for all that your new life has brought you, including the challenges! You'll grow and learn more than you've ever imagined. Spend lots of time talking to God, and in those sacred moments, remember all that you've been given.

Fill your heart what you choose. Reach out to your husband and stepkids and let them become a part of you. The more involved you are with their lives, the more care and compassion you'll feel. The feelings of family and devotion in your heart will help to push out the resentment. You will become stronger and feel more in control of your life, more able to give generously and seek what you need from those around you.

> *So let each one give as he purposes in his heart, not grudgingly or of necessity; for God loves a cheerful giver.*
> —2 Corinthians 9:7 (NKJV)

 *To Think About* _____

Take your time to complete answers to each of the following questions.

What is the biggest source of your resentment?

Who do you need to talk to about your resentment?

How can you fill your heart more to help overcome the resentment plaguing it?

How will you ask God to help you understand and reconcile your feelings?

To God in Prayer

L ord, thank You for holding my hand through these difficult times. Please help me to remove these draining feelings from my heart and mind. Help me to find the comfort and solace I need in my family, and please help my husband and stepchildren to understand my feelings. Please help me to overcome my resentment and plant love, patience, and compassion in its place. Amen.

God's Response

If God encouraged you in some specific way, use this space to record His response.

CHAPTER EIGHT

MANAGING RESPONSIBILITY

And God is able to make all grace abound to you, so that in all things at all times, having all that you need, you will abound in every good work.

—*2 Corinthians 9:8 (NIV)*

*T*hings get busy quickly in a stepfamily, don't they?! Everything you're responsible for can be a big load. Often your responsibilities come unexpectedly and can double or triple instantly. Your stepkids could come to live with you, for example, and you would go from an every-other-weekend stepmom to a full-time mom in their lives. Or, your financial contributions may be needed to meet child support payments, or you may be expected to drop your plans, in order to accommodate the kids' changing needs.

Maybe it's not a dramatic shift in responsibility that's weighing you down, but just the everyday demands that stepmotherhood places on you. It's time for prayer when the load is heavy. And God is there, with an answer.

Why are you downcast, O my soul? Why so disturbed within me? Put your hope in God, for I will yet praise him, my Savior and my God.

—*Psalm 42:5 (NIV)*

You don't have to carry all of your responsibilities alone. Just knowing that God will hold everything on His broad shoulders is enough to get your focus off the terrifying demands and onto His unfailing faithfulness. He knows you can't handle all of the things this life brings without Him, and that's why He is always right beside you.

When you know He is there, you can forge a real-world plan for managing your responsibilities. You can look at every demand as simply a part of life that you're getting under control. When you and God are working together on your plan, you can't lose.

Try this five-step guide to get you going.

> *W*HEN YOU AND GOD ARE WORKING TOGETHER ON YOUR PLAN, YOU CAN'T LOSE.

1. Set Limits

God is your constant companion, but you are only one flesh-and-blood person, so you have to set some limits. Don't allow more into your life than you can handle. I know that sounds impossible, especially if you're the stepmom about to become a full-time mom, but what I mean here is not based on the facts of your life, but your *response* to them.

There are two parts to this step. First, don't start something you can't or don't want to continue. Does that mean you shouldn't ever make a kind gesture or go beyond the call once in a while? No, but you don't have to become everyone's dumping ground or keeper either. You have to retain control of your time and your sanity or you won't get through the difficult and onto the delightful.

Second, if you've already allowed yourself to be obligated against your will, and it's too much, you are the only person who can stop it. Say that over and over to yourself until you believe it. No one is going to save you but *you*. And here's how: it's a matter of holding on and letting go. That's step 2.

2. Identify Your Priorities

You will find the time, energy, and resources for what you love and for what you want. It's that simple. Then the responsibility associated with everything you love and want in your life won't be a burden, but just a part of who you are now. When you know which responsibilities match with your priorities and which ones don't, you can hold on to the ones you want and let go of the others.

That approach makes sense for you and everybody else in your family. When you focus on what you handle best, everyone benefits. When you stray or allow others to pull you from God's priorities for your life, everyone loses.

> *There are different kinds of gifts, but the same Spirit. There are different kinds of service, but the same Lord. There are different kinds of working, but the same God works all of them in all men.*
>
> *—1 Corinthians 12:4–6 (NIV)*

3. Consider Responsibilities as Opportunities

Consider the responsibilities you do accept as opportunities to shine! Approach them with God by your side, with a renewed sense of purpose and understanding. Every responsibility, no matter how mundane it is, is a way to interact with and witness for the Lord, as everything is for "the glory of God" (1 Corinthians 10:31 NIV).

Talk to Him during your work every day. If your responsibilities are overwhelming, ask Him to show you how to handle them better. Maybe there's a skill you can learn that will help you, or maybe there's a way to share the load with someone else. The goal doesn't have to be to rid yourself of all responsibility, but to become more efficient at managing it. Then you are ready for another aspect of meeting your responsibilities: you become a teacher for those around you. That's the next step.

4. Teach Responsibility by Example

Realize that we teach far more by our example than by our language. When we have our priorities in order and we meet the responsibilities associated with them with grace and courage, we show everyone the strength and resolve that comes from God. You don't have to be a superhero or a martyr. You just need to live in your stepmom role, at your pace, achieving your goals, and with the Lord at your side.

When you model that example for everyone in your life, you're meeting one of your most important responsibilities without even realizing it. What a blessing!

5. When Overwhelmed, Return to Step 1

Even when your intentions are good and your priorities are in order, your role can still be overwhelming any day, any time. Remember through the struggles not to lose heart, not to give up, not to abandon your hope. When your responsibilities get out of hand, go back to step 1, reorganize or readjust to accommodate the circumstances, and carry on. But always know deep in your heart that you are strong enough to meet whatever happens.

It's true that the Lord will not give us more than we can handle. It's also true that He gave us the good sense to know when we're getting in too deeply. Remember that you can't save the world, but can make a significant difference in your little corner of it when you know what matters to you and you meet those responsibilities willingly and with God's blessing. You will find great joy and peace in your journey working through the priorities you and God choose for your life. Enjoy everything that comes with them, one day at a time.

*Therefore do not worry about tomorrow, for tomorrow will
worry about itself. Each day has enough trouble of its own.*
                                        —*Matthew 6:34 (NIV)*

To Think About _____

Take your time to complete answers to each of the following questions.

Who has been setting the priorities in your life?

How have you felt overwhelmed by your responsibilities, and
what can you do today to manage them better?

How can you reframe your responsibilities in God's view and
find a renewed strength?

To God in Prayer

Lord, I come to You burdened and overwhelmed. Please help me to step back, look into my heart and Yours, and know what matters as I search for the best use of my time and talents. Please help me to meet my responsibilities in a way that reflects You. Please make me strong enough for each day. Amen.

God's Response

If God encouraged you in some specific way, use this space to record His response.

CHAPTER NINE

ESCAPING DESPAIR

The righteous cry out, and the Lord hears them; he delivers them from all their troubles. The Lord is close to the brokenhearted and saves those who are crushed in spirit.
—Psalm 34:17–18 (NIV)

*I*t was never supposed to be like this—so very, very hard! We've all been there, deep in the underworld of our own despair. Maybe your husband can't see what you're going through. Maybe the kids won't accept you. Maybe their mom is disrupting your life or overstepping her bounds.

You try and you try, but what keeps coming to your lips and your heart is only one thought: *"I can't do this anymore!"*

Have you ever screamed that, or just dared to feel it? Have you ever been so upset and saddened by your life's circumstances that you thought you couldn't go on? Have you ever been afraid that you'd never survive the role of stepmom? If you've ever thought that this life is just too hard, too much work, too much risk, you're not alone.

You're not destined to navigate the strangling waters by yourself either. Your despair is understandable. The Lord's help is near. For right now, don't worry about doing anything, simply listen.

God is our refuge and strength, a very present help in trouble. Therefore we will not fear, though the earth be removed, and though the mountains be carried into the midst of the sea; though its waters roar and be troubled, though the mountains shake with its swelling.

                                   Psalm 46:1–3 (NKJV)

Settle Down and Listen

Listen to your heart. I know it sounds crazy, but go ahead and accept the pain that you feel. You can't deal with it until you face it. Sometimes we don't want to feel the desperation and hopelessness. We don't want to admit that we are not happy or successful. But go ahead and acknowledge everything that you feel. You can't change your situation until you're clear about what it is.

Listen to your mind. Sounds a little backward, doesn't it? It makes sense, though. What do you spend your time thinking about? Are you plagued with thoughts of regret, anger, or even hatred? Or do you spend your time thinking about the good moments of your life, despite the challenges, and the bright future that will come if you can hold on?

Sometimes, the desperate thoughts are just moments that will pass, not the prevailing nature of your life. Sometimes, they are the only things you can hear. Decide which kind of desperation you're in, and then reach for the person closest to you for help.

Listen to your husband. Maybe he's feeling the same thing, having the same worries or fears, or maybe he can explain yours to you. Maybe he can help you see another side of the suffocation you feel. Much of your stepfamily's success is based on your ability to communicate clearly with your husband, to get past your fears and talk openly and honestly.

Ask him to tell you what he hears you saying, and then listen to him. Maybe you've let your worries get out of control.

Maybe things aren't as bad as they seem. Or maybe he'll understand exactly what parts of your life are so hard and become the support you need. Don't be afraid to level with him about your desperation. If you hold it in, it will only grow.

Most importantly, listen to the Lord. Stop trying to solve everything for a moment and just listen. What is He telling you? He is likely trying to comfort and sustain you. He is probably wanting you to stop looking at all the bad and start looking at Him to help you find the good. He is wanting you to succeed, and He is willing to start over at the very beginning with you, if that's what it takes.

> *Be still and know that I am God.*
>
> *—Psalm 46:10 (NKJV)*

When in desperation you're ready to give up, sometimes the beginning is the best place to start. Go back to when you didn't know what your family life would bring. Go back to the time when you were optimistic and positive, when you didn't feel the weight of a thousand hurts on your heart. Then let God carry you through today with an optimistic and positive outlook. Replace one bad thought with one good one, and then rest.

When the despair is heavy, you will be exhausted. You will need to mend and recover before you can fix what's broken. That's OK. Your family isn't going anywhere in a day or a week. Take some time to rest in the Lord's arms and recover your sense of well-being.

> *"Come to me, all you who are weary and burdened, and I will give you rest. Take my yoke upon you and learn from me, for I am gentle and humble in heart, and you will find rest for your souls."*
>
> *—Matthew 11:28–29 (NIV)*

Reacquaint yourself with your personal walk with God, with the peace that He alone gives. Spend time with Him just listening, not trying to accomplish anything, but resting and recovering in His warmth and compassion. Give yourself time to repair and rejuvenate your heart. Strengthen yourself with everything that He is so that you can give everything you are to your family and your future.

LISTEN DAILY

As you work to pull yourself out of the pit you're in, look at each crisis as one isolated event. Don't lump everything together into a "terrible awful mistake of a life," or you will never see the possibility of peace again. You don't have to "heal and be healed" this very second. That pressure and obligation helps lead to desperation. Let go of the urgency that you feel to fix everything at once. Take care of things, one at a time, with the Lord by your side. Then your despair melts away because it's replaced by His encouragement and companionship.

Just being encouraged instead of enraged about what is to come goes a long way in a stepfamily. Encourage yourself by believing that God will forever hold you close, no matter what, and that He'll equip you with everything you need to leave your despair behind so that you can go on to happier times—always in His arms.

To Think About _____

Take your time to complete answers to each of the following questions.

What one thing can you do today that will encourage you and help alleviate your feelings of despair? If you don't know the answer, go to God in prayer, and He will reveal it to you.

How will you talk to your husband today so that he sees more of how you feel?

What are you missing by spending so much time with desperate thoughts?

How can you change that, starting today?

To God in Prayer

*L*ord, please help me with these suffocating feelings of despair. I want to be calm and confident in my role, and I need Your support through the times I don't understand and can't control. Please stay close, heal my broken spirit, encourage me with Your strength, and guide me to a more satisfying and peaceful life. Amen.

God's Response

If God encouraged you in some specific way, use this space to record His response.

Chapter Ten

Trading in the Envy

Search me, O God, and know my heart; test me and know
my anxious thoughts. See if there is any offensive way in me,
and lead me in the way everlasting.
—*Psalm 139:23–24 (NIV)*

When we are feeling envious, we simply cannot pay attention to what's most important in our lives. We lose sight of the questions we need to ask ourselves about how we spend our time and energy, and our growth as stepmoms stops dead still. Our future is in danger when we let the habit of envy color our world. It will never get us where we want to be.

Envy is a particularly debilitating emotion, unique and powerful in its ability to hurt you. It gnaws at your heart and soul because it focuses your attention away from the blessings you've been given (material or otherwise) and onto what you see of someone else's life. That focus is especially detrimental to a stepmom because we often find ourselves with less than those around us, certainly less money and fewer possessions.

When the focus is on what we *don't* have instead of what we *do*, our vision is polluted. With the envy in our eyes, we won't ever see what wonderful blessings God has already given us and the ones He has in store for us. It's a sad way to live.

THE SOURCE

Why is envy such a problem in a stepmom's life? The answer probably lies in the many things that we feel we have lost

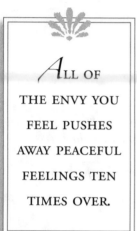

because of our choice to become a stepmom. Because a stepfamily always seems to have to swim against the tide to survive, it's common for a stepmom to long for a simpler, less draining, more comfortable life.

In that vein, one of the easiest things for us to do is compare our life to that of our husband's former wife. If you're living through tight finances and broken plans because of her, it can seem almost natural to hate what can feel like captivity and envy everything your stepkids' mom has at your husband's expense. If you're raising her children (with or without their consent), it's hard not to feel overwhelmed at what should be her responsibility. It's easy to envy her wealth or her freedom, but it hurts only one person—*you.*

THE RESULT

All envy comes from not being satisfied with where you are, and it just shows itself by focusing on where *others* are. You waste valuable time and energy when you choose to make someone else's life more important than your own. When you let what your stepkids' mom has bother you so much that you can't see what you have, you've made your life miserable all by yourself. All of the envy you feel pushes away peaceful feelings ten times over. The result is decay from within.

> *A heart at peace gives life to the body, but envy rots the bones.*
> —*Proverbs 14:30 (NIV)*

We need every ounce of strength we can muster to fight this dangerous emotion and get through our other steplife problems. A set of rotting bones to hold us up won't help us very much, now, will it?! We can take that verse literally (because we do need our physical strength), but the "rotting bones" of your heart are far more important. The strength that you have in your heart is eroded when you let envy in. Keep envy out and you can experience a life of peace.

The Method

But what do you do to keep envy away? You change your focus from someone else's life to your own. You change your focus from what you've lost to what you've gained. You change your focus from where you've failed to where you can succeed. Making the changes that you need in your life to create more happiness and satisfaction will leave no room for envy. There will be far greater joys.

> *"Do not store up for yourselves treasures on earth, where moth and rust destroy, and where thieves break in and steal. But store up for yourselves treasures in heaven, where moth and rust do not destroy, and where thieves do not break in and steal. For where your treasure is, there your heart will be also."*
>
> *—Matthew 6:19–21 (NIV)*

The treasures that will bring you the most happiness aren't the ones you can buy, or the ones that come from someone else's loss. What others do or don't do, have or don't have, is irrelevant. It's what happens inside *your* home and *your* heart that matters. If you will be envious for anything, let it be for the closeness and family connectedness that only time will allow. Let your longing for those kinds of treasures propel you to reach them hand in hand with God to guide your way. Those are the blessings God has in store for us.

Create and remember special times that you and your husband share. Etch in your heart the connections that you and your stepchild feel, even the slightest ones. Write about the deepening relationship you have with the Lord, and that action alone will replace any misplaced desires that offer no comfort. The life that someone else has, even if it's filled with mansions of gold, means nothing to you. It can't hurt you unless you let it. Turn your mind and your heart away from there and toward the life you truly want.

> *If we live in the Spirit, let us also walk in the Spirit. Let us not become conceited, provoking one another, envying one another.*
>
>   —*Galatians 5:25–26 (NKJV)*

A WONDERFUL BLESSING

A wonderful thing will happen when you keep envy away from your heart. The beauty of a simpler life will find you. Your mind will not be cluttered with the unimportant trappings that envy shoves into your heart. The more you move your focus away from wanting what someone else has, the more happiness you'll find in the bounty of what you have and what you can create. Without envy to guide you, you simply make the choices that benefit you and your walk with God.

But when your life is ruled by envy, disorder prevails because envy is always pushing you somewhere that isn't good for you, pushing you to destroy instead of build. "For where you have envy and selfish ambition, there you find disorder and every evil practice" (James 3:16 NIV).

That's no way for a stepmom to live. We need lots of order! We need to always find the purest truth, the clearest path, the strongest conviction. We can't do that with an envious heart that scrambles everything around us, causing us to turn our "what's important" list upside down. The simplicity in a life without envy will make everything clear again. The choice is only between what's good for you and your family and what isn't. It's not hard to decide.

To Think About _____

Take your time to complete answers to each of the following questions.

What situations or thoughts make you particularly envious, and how can you avoid them?

What part of being a stepmom can you fill with peace so that envy cannot take hold?

Can you try getting to know your stepkids' mom a bit better so the two of you can understand each other's lives and maybe join forces instead of battling envy and hostility?

Pray for the clarity to see the amazing life that God has in store just for you.

To God in Prayer

Lord, I cannot hide these envious feelings from You, and I am ashamed. Please help me to direct my focus from someone else's life onto my own and to understand Your unique purpose for the wife and stepmom I am. Help me to appreciate the treasures of my family and to join with You in creating a life full of the blessings we can only have together. I pray that I will feel Your peace that can banish even the tiniest speck of envy. Please help me see what is truly important in this life You have given me. Amen.

God's Response

If God encouraged you in some specific way, use this space to record His response.

A Stepmom Prays . . .

I had a hard time trying to overcome being envious of my husband's former wife. I constantly compared myself to her and felt discouraged and frustrated. I started praying, and God helped me open my eyes to the wonderful blessings that were in front of me all along. I have a wonderful husband, three loving children, and a beautiful house. I finally started appreciating the things that I took for granted.

I still may struggle from time to time, but I try to stay focused and continue to ask for God's hand in helping me.

—**Kimberly**, stepmom of two, mom of one

A Stepmom Prays . . .

Resentment is a strange thing. It doesn't really exist on its own; it is created in the mind of those who feel they are wronged by another's actions. It then becomes a magnet, collecting negative feelings resulting from incidents that are often completely unrelated.

For many years, these feelings of resentment controlled my life. It took a very long time for me to recognize that the negative feelings I was having toward my stepsons had *nothing* to do with them.

One particularly frustrating day, I made the choice to have faith, and I prayed for guidance in dealing with daily drudgery that seemed so insignificant, but was deeply affecting my happiness. I began to face the resentment for what it was. It soon became clear to me that my stepsons leaving their dirty socks in the living room had nothing to do with their mother buying a new car when she claimed she couldn't afford to pay child support.

God answered my prayers and gave me the strength to not only separate these feelings and deal with them individually, but He seems to have also provided me with a new and very important skill: to not utter one single word about mislaid dirty socks. Our house is a much more loving place these days.

—**Sue L.**, Oregon, mother of one, stepmother of two

Peace in the Struggle

Steplife has a way of throwing you into situations you'd never ask for and then expecting you to be gracious about it. Maybe you know that feeling when you see a struggle coming and wonder how you'll get through it. Somehow, it always works out.

When my stepsons' mom's dad was seriously ill in the hospital far from home, the boys were with us around the clock, and their mom and I did most of the talking on the telephone. We were cordial to each other at the time, but you wouldn't have called us friends.

Then our lives put us together in an unforeseen way, and she may have been as surprised as I was to hear her say she was glad her boys were with me. We both struggled through the difficult time, her with her family and me trying to do what I could for our boys.

After her father died and she was home again, she sent me a lovely plant with a card that read simply, "Thank you so much." I still have it. And I'm thankful, too, for everything that awaits and blesses us, on the other side of our struggles.

Coping

Each one should test his own actions.
Then he can take pride
in himself, without comparing
himself to somebody else.
—Galatians 6:4 (NIV)

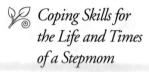 *Coping Skills for
the Life and Times
of a Stepmom*

- *Honesty*
- *Courage*
- *Understanding*
- *Forgiveness*
- *Acceptance*

Coping

Coping with life as a stepmom is an amazing walk with God. As we turn to Him for help and instruction and learn to model His approach and responses to every situation, we mature in a way that touches everything we do.

As we depend on the Lord to be right beside us, we trust ourselves to trust Him, to let Him be our guide. We know we can't cope with our lives alone, and we learn quickly that only through His love and grace can we weather the storms we can neither predict nor control.

We probably will struggle through moments of stepmotherhood always, but when we allow the Lord to teach us how to act and react, we find less struggling and more progress. We find an inner strength to work through our challenges, a strength based on time with and dependence on God.

We find that we cope so much better when we look inward first, when we focus our energies on what we can control, on what we can learn and give, and on how we can stay true to ourselves and build our families at the same time.

The Lord wants a part in our steplives. When we go to Him with all the confusion and trauma, we see that He is standing right there, waiting and ready to give us the logic, compassion, ability, discipline, and integrity to carry on. *He* is the reason we can cope with the choices we've made, cope with the choices of others, and learn to make better choices from now on.

God loves us so much. It is His pleasure and His work to steer us through everything that's tough. He delights in our learning, our trust, and our submission to Him. We find sanctuary and guidance every time we ask.

Chapter Eleven

Living Honestly

The LORD is near to all who call upon Him, to all who call upon Him in truth. He will fulfill the desire of those who fear Him; He also will hear their cry and save them.
—Psalm 145:18–19 (NKJV)

*F*or many reasons, honesty can be one of the hardest concepts to find in a stepfamily. Everyone's feelings are raw and fluid, and the wide range of emotions can lead to dishonesty. Sometimes, the kids aren't honest about how they feel or the things they do. You may find that your husband isn't being honest about his feelings, or you may be tormented by lies from your stepkids' mom. All of that kind of dishonesty can put you under a terrible strain.

Sadly, a magic remedy for any of the dishonesty you face is not within your control. But the honesty that you *can* control is more important. It's more than just telling the truth: it's the way you live your life—as a stepmom, as a woman, as an example to all those around you, and as a testament to your Lord.

If that kind of honesty seems hard to grasp amid the challenges of your life, don't worry. The Lord has given you the perfect example and instruction.

*"If you abide in My word, you are My disciples indeed.
And you shall know the truth, and the truth shall make
you free."*

—John 8:31–32 (NKJV)

Abiding in the Word and
Reflecting the Lord

When we abide in the Lord's Word, we can't help but understand and reflect Him in an honest way. He will never lie or misrepresent Himself to us, and in that indisputable truth, we know all we need to know. We know about His love, compassion, and character. We have the basis we need to be honest in our lives.

*T*HERE
IS NO ROOM
FOR FEAR.

With the comfort and joy that comes from a deepening relationship with the Lord, you will feel the pull to honesty in everything you do and say. When we let Him into our broken and complicated lives and bare our true souls, we experience freedom and inspiration to live His ways in all of our earthly relationships, even the difficult stepfamily ones. There is no room for fear.

We can and will find the strength to be honest in every single part of our lives. Sometimes, that's scary for a stepmom, but it doesn't have to be. When things are tough, you can remain honest and enjoy the benefits of that choice. Here's how.

Relying on the Lord

When you abide in the Lord's Word, you learn who He is, and you learn that He never changes. When you claim this loving fact, you can apply it to your life and use Him as a model for everything you do.

*Those who know your name will trust in you, for you,
Lord, have never forsaken those who seek you.*
                                        —Psalm 9:10 (NIV)

Because God is always the same, you don't ever have to doubt
Him. That knowledge supports everything else that you think
about Him. Let it be the same with you. If you tell your stepkids
the truth and apply discipline consistently, even if they won't
like it, they will learn to use your honesty as a frame of reference.
If you react in the same way every time you have an encounter
with their mom, she will learn that you can't be influenced by
her antics because of your strong determination to remain true
to yourself and your convictions.

When you rely on God as your example, you can live your
life honestly even in the difficult situations. When you make it
your goal to reflect the Lord, He will graciously supply you with
the grace to meet your challenges every day. "Let your conversation be always full of grace, seasoned with salt, so that you may
know how to answer everyone" (Colossians 4:6 NIV).

Just as salt is a complement to our food, our honest reflec-
tion of Christ through our words will complement our stepmom
role. As we more effectively communicate with people around
us, our job will be easier. When we live our lives in a way that is
honest, sincere, and based on God's example, we eliminate a lot
of problems just like that, in a snap, regardless of what everyone
else around us does.

BLESSINGS OF HONESTY

When you make the conscious choice to live your life in an honest way, you'll find all kinds of blessings. Let's look at just two.

You build integrity. Everyone has a lot to learn about everyone else in a stepfamily. People without the benefit of history
or blood have to come together in another way and try to form
a family. Suspicions may run high while everyone assesses the

motives of everyone else, and getting to know one another takes time. You help that process along when you honestly present yourself to your family members.

When you tell the truth every time, when your actions match your words, when you make choices that are right and pure—when you are honest with everyone about who you are and what you stand for—it won't take long for everyone to know you well. When your integrity is your compass and your example is God, you are a stepmom with great strength and power. Once your family recognizes that integrity in you, it only makes you stronger.

You move forward. One most unfortunate by-product of a dishonest life is the inability to move forward and enjoy all of the wonderful blessings God has planned for you. If your time and energy is tied up in trying to cover lies or be something you're not, you can't be the kind of stepmom you want to be. Living dishonestly means living in the past, because you can't go forward without a clear conscience and a clear vision of what you want out of your stepmom role. You can only have a clear conscience and a clear vision when you make the choice for honesty.

> *Instead, speaking the truth in love, we will in all things grow up into him who is the Head, that is, Christ.*
> —Ephesians 4:15 (NIV)

Once you've established a habit and a pattern of honesty, you can base the future on that as well. You can look forward to exciting plans that are true to who you are and to continued instruction and companionship with God through any trials you face. You can go forward with complete confidence in yourself to handle whatever happens because the truth of *who you are* and *who God is*, is enough. You are free to pursue your dreams and reach great heights in stepmotherhood when you have only an honest foundation on which to build. There is no other way.

🌿 *To Think About* _____

Take your time to complete answers to each of the following questions.

Have you been dishonest in the way you've played your step-mom role?

What are the hardest parts about living honestly in your step-family?

How will you begin to build your integrity today?

Go to God with your concerns and follow His lead in all situations to come. Will you commit to this?

To God in Prayer

Lord, please help me to abide in You, to take Your truth and apply it to my life. Please help me to speak honestly, to behave honestly, and to choose honesty in every opportunity so that I may reflect You in everything I do. Help me to show my character and integrity to my family every day. Guide me in my choices, and remind me constantly that Your truth leads to my truth, and only in a safe haven of honesty can we have the greatest freedom to live a bountiful life. Thank You for Your example. Amen.

God's Response

If God encouraged you in some specific way, use this space to record His response.

CHAPTER TWELVE

PRACTICING COURAGE

You, O Lord, keep my lamp burning; my God turns my darkness into light. With your help I can advance against a troop; with my God I can scale a wall.

—Psalm 18:28–29 (NIV)

*D*id you have any idea that being a stepmom would require so much courage? It's amazing how brave you have to be to succeed in this role. Even more amazing is that you can always rise to the occasion; you can always manage to see through the clutter and learn what you need to know and reach the solution you need. Do you know where that courage comes from? There's only one place.

The Lord is kind and merciful, and to us stepmoms, who are surely a pitiful bunch at times, He doles out the courage by the bucketfuls. He holds us up when we think we'll fall. He catches us when we do. He shows us the path we should take, and then gives us the courage and words and wisdom to pursue it.

WHEN YOU NEED IT

How can you be sure that the Lord will give you the courage you need? Why wouldn't He? It gives Him no pleasure to see you fearful and lost. When you have to speak your mind about your stepkids' behavior, for example, you'll be able to take a deep breath and say what you need to say. When you attempt to befriend your stepkids' mom, you'll find a way to extend your-self to her. When you need to talk to your husband about your family's problems, you'll be able to because you know that even though ignoring them is easier, it is also detrimental.

When you try time and time again to reach the stepchild who rejects you, when you open your heart to a life that is nothing you ever planned, when you accept a past that colors your present and your future—that's when you're drawing on the unbelievable courage that you have deep inside because of God. He is near.

> *Draw near to God and He will draw near to you.*
> —*James 4:8 (NKJV)*

What It Gives You

When you go forward into all of those difficult situations with a courageous heart, you open yourself up to a wealth of bless-ings untold. You promote an environment of understanding and growth where nothing is stagnant because of fear, and everything good is a possibility. "And let us not grow weary while doing good, for in due season we shall reap if we do not lose heart" (Galatians 6:9 NKJV).

Stepmothering requires bold thoughts and bold actions. You have to be courageous in your mind and in your heart. You have to be willing to put yourself on the line every day, to open up to others and to protect yourself. I know that sounds contradictory, but it's not.

Courage in Practice

The courage to bare your heart is the courage to be who you are in your family, the courage to face your challenges each day by relying on your mind, abilities, talents, and compassion for everyone in your home—and to trust that you can supply whatever is needed. You have what you need because God gives it to you. Because He is pouring in the courage as quickly as you need it, you'll never run out. You'll always have the exact amount you need for *your* heart and *your* family.

The courage to protect yourself is the courage to know what you need and then see that you get it, so that you can build the life you want. Everybody in a stepfamily is needy, and it's not uncommon for a stepmom to over-look or minimize her needs as she tries to take care of everyone else. It takes great courage to ask for what you need and to set boundaries to protect your heart and home, but it is essential.

It takes great courage to ask for what you need, and to set boundaries.

When you are courageous enough to protect yourself, you become stron-ger and more capable of protecting your entire family. God wants you to feel safe, secure, and protected so that you can easily claim the courage you'll need to meet your challenges. So let Him show you how to protect yourself so that you *can* share yourself. It works together, and it works because God will never leave you ill-equipped for anything you need to do. You can be brave, because He already is.

> *Do you not know? Have you not heard? The Lord is the everlasting God, the Creator of the ends of the earth. He will not grow tired or weary, and his understanding no one can fathom. He gives strength to the weary and increases the power of the weak.*
>
> —*Isaiah 40:28–29 (NIV)*

To Think About _____

Take your time to complete answers to each of the following questions.

When have you felt that you had no courage?

What made you feel that way?

How has stepmotherhood made you question your courage?

When do you feel the most courageous? Duplicate those circumstances as much as possible and ask God to help you breathe His courage into every moment of your life.

How will you protect and bare your heart today?

To God in Prayer

L ord, sometimes I think my courage has disappeared, and yet, my life calls for me to be brave every moment. Please help me tap into Your courage and go forward strong and capable to all I need to do. Please stay close to me and never let me fear my mission or question Your devotion to me. Amen.

God's Response

If God encouraged you in some specific way, use this space to record His response.

CHAPTER THIRTEEN

GAINING UNDERSTANDING

"Call to Me, and I will answer you, and show you great and mighty things, which you do not know."

—*Jeremiah 33:3 (NKJV)*

Coping successfully with life as a stepmom takes more wisdom and understanding than any of us could have ever imagined. We go through those stages of shock and disbelief, grief and confusion, and we make our way to a workable strategy for dealing with our steplives. Some things we learn quickly, and others, well, let's just say that the Lord has to put in a little over-time with our stubborn hearts!

UNDERSTANDING OURSELVES

As we settle into our stepfamilies, we want so much to understand all the changes and challenges, lessons and logic of what's happening to us. Sometimes, if we've come from a background where things seemed to make sense most of the time, dealing with a life that often doesn't is tough. We feel inadequate, defeated, burdened, and lost. If we could just understand everything and everyone, we think we could manage. But we have to start with ourselves.

When we take the time to learn, it's amazing what the Lord will reveal to help us through difficult times. We begin by looking *inside.* As we define our motives and dreams, we realize what's most important to us. Identifying what stresses us and pushes us into a black hole of despair helps us structure our lives. Simply by understanding ourselves, we can work with everyone else more effectively. When we learn to identify our feelings, then we know how to deal with them.

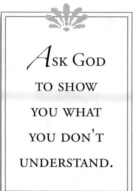

*A*SK GOD TO SHOW YOU WHAT YOU DON'T UNDERSTAND.

It's hard to understand all the emotions going around in our heads and hearts for several reasons. Sometimes, one feeling may mask something else. And sometimes, we don't want to admit or acknowledge the unkind feelings that consume us. Our difficult feelings won't make God move away from us; in fact, He stays close to help us understand them so we can find the happiness and peace we crave.

Peace in your life isn't about burying your head in the sand until someone changes to meet your specifications. It's about understanding everything you can so that you can make changes *yourself,* in order to make things better.

WISDOM FROM GOD

What don't you understand? I know, silly question, but humor me. Keep a record of the feelings and situations that puzzle and frustrate you. Note the circumstances around your times of stress and confusion. Ask God to show you what you don't understand.

> *How much better to get wisdom than gold, to choose under-standing rather than silver!*
>
> —*Proverbs 16:16 (NIV)*

Put every ounce of effort you have into learning about your steplife through God's eyes. Ask Him what He sees so that you might open your eyes to possibilities you've missed. Give God all your questions. Pray for His answers, and watch for everything He will reveal to you. Turn everything over to Him as a classroom, a laboratory, and prepare for His guidance.

You can do this starting today. The next situation you face that has you scratching your head, go to the Lord with it first. Empty your mind of every preconceived notion, and listen for His direction. Do what He instructs, and then listen for the next direction. Learn from Him one command at a time.

UNDERSTANDING YOUR ROLE

We all have to learn how to be stepmoms. It can take years. We actually never stop learning, and we have to constantly adjust to the many outside factors that influence our lives. But regardless of others' choices, we have to focus on what *we* can do.

The more you understand about your role, the more progress you can make with it. If your stepkids are heavily influenced against you by their mom, for example, learn how to work within the limits you have and to accept that you may have to wait until they are older to build a greater relationship with them. Or, if you are the everyday mom to your stepkids, learn how to do that without losing yourself in the process. And if you share your stepkids with their mom, learn how to do so graciously, to understand your place while respecting hers.

Any of these situations, and all the others you face, requires more negotiating, compromise, and understanding than a major-league contract, but the Lord *will* guide you each step of the way every day. When you understand where you fit into your family, you know how to maximize yourself. You know how to make things better for yourself and everyone else too.

UNDERSTANDING YOUR RELATIONSHIP WITH YOUR HUSBAND

In a stepfamily, a previous relationship or marriage can have an impact on your relationship with your husband. You might think that his past wouldn't hurt you or that he would always be able to separate his bad history from this marriage with you today. But that is not always the case.

Understanding the life he had before you will help you deal with the problems you have now. Knowing that your husband may have some insecurities of his own, for example, will help you deal with him if he jumps to conclusions or misinterprets your actions. Pause and study his motivation before you react in anger; you may avoid some arguments and even help him over his fears.

If you understand his motives or responses—even if you don't agree with them—you have a better frame of reference from which to discuss a delicate topic. Ask God to show you how to talk to your husband about your relationship. Ask Him to show you these possibilities and grant you the compassion to handle the problems more effectively. That's all possible because of *your* growth in understanding.

UNDERSTANDING DIFFICULT SITUATIONS

The life of a stepmom is filled with the most bizarre situations and unbelievable experiences. You'll find yourself shaking your head sometimes, wondering how people can behave the way they do and how you can find yourself in such trying predicaments day after day. The baffling behavior of former wives or stepkids can make you feel powerless and confused, unsure how to respond.

You may fight the situation, frustrated at the insanity of, for example, a former wife who delights in trying to alienate her kids from you. Even if you understand her motives, you're still faced with handling the situation, with understanding what you can do to overcome the assault. You may be able to change her behavior one day, but more importantly, you will learn how to respond to it by following God's Word and by holding on to your integrity.

When we understand that nothing these other people do will change God's control of our lives, we can go on as He would have us go. When we go to Him for our strength and direction, we find the solace and security we need to deal with those who create havoc in our lives. And what does He tell us to do? To "put on His armor" and prepare for any battle that arises.

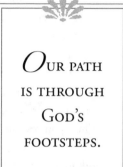

Our path is through God's footsteps.

> *Therefore put on the full armor of God, so that when the day of evil comes, you may be able to stand your ground, and after you have done everything, to stand.*
> *—Ephesians 6:13 (NIV)*

When we understand how protected we are with His words of truth, the chaos others cause becomes far less important than we thought it was. It is still real and painful, of course, but our path is through God's footsteps, in holding on to Him through the storm and not wallowing in what hurts. Would He tell us to retaliate, to hurt others as they have hurt us? No, He would use the situations created by others to draw us closer to Him in prayer.

LEARNING STILL

We may never understand the choices someone else makes, but we know that the choice God directs us to will never be hard to understand and never cause us more pain. Every moment leads to more understanding when we continually talk with God.

Seek to know the little things, and the big things will make more sense too. Let Him guide you in the right direction when you're faced with an incomprehensible situation, and be true to your spirit that rests in Him.

Know that you don't have to respond to every situation you face with the same anger or vindictiveness directed toward you. You can maintain your standard of behavior even if others are losing theirs. As you seek to understand, you will reap the benefits, but nothing will get any better if you try to "win." When you respond with poor words or actions that don't reflect God in your life, you'll never get the satisfaction you want or end an argument well. Remember: understanding that patterns God's example is always the better choice.

> *I will bless the* Lord *who has given me counsel; my heart also instructs me in the night seasons. I have set the Lord always before me; because He is at my right hand I shall not be moved.*
>
> *—Psalm 16:7–8 (NKJV)*

To Think About _____

Take your time to complete answers to each of the following questions.

Who is the most difficult person in your steplife to understand?

How can you apply God's teaching to help you understand yourself and others better?

How have you reacted out of pain or anger instead of understanding in the past?

What has it cost you, and how will you change that approach?

To God in Prayer

*L*ord, I pray for understanding in this very confusing role I live. Please help me to learn from the past, be more careful in my responses, and rely on Your control every day. Please help me to understand myself so that I can find my way to the peace I need. Please help me understand my life so that I can do my part to make my and my family's life better. Amen.

God's Response

If God encouraged you in some specific way, use this space to record His response.

CHAPTER FOURTEEN

SHOWING FORGIVENESS

Bear with each other and forgive whatever grievances you may have against one another. Forgive as the Lord forgave you.

Colossians 3:13 (NIV)

*F*orgiveness is an important blessing in our lives, no matter what is going on around us or how impossible our step situations are. It's healing, renewing, and freeing, and it eventually touches everything we do. Forgiveness is both a skill learned and a gift received for every stepmom.

PRACTICING THE SKILL

You learn to forgive with practice and with a choice. The Lord knows how to forgive us without hesitation, eagerly blotting out our failures when we humbly ask. We, on the other hand, may not have anyone who offends us ask for our forgiveness, humbly or otherwise. It doesn't matter. We can forgive *anyway,* if we want to. The process has two parts that work together toward something far better than a heavy grudge.

First, separate the person who hurt you from the hurt in your heart. You can choose to forgive the person without forgetting about the pain—the two don't have to come together. If your stepchild is unkind to you, you can forgive him or her by understanding that behavior is only a part of a whole person who sinned or made a mistake. You need to be able to interact with your stepchild, so you forgive, giving yourself a chance for progress that you wouldn't have if you didn't move away from the hurt.

> *Get rid of all bitterness, rage and anger, brawling and slander, along with every form of malice. Be kind and compassionate to one another, forgiving each other, just as in Christ God forgave you.*
>
> —*Ephesians 4:31–32 (NIV)*

At the same time, you can work your way through the behavior. You can heal from the pain and allow yourself to put it in the past, in time. This experience in regeneration is a remarkable teacher.

FORGIVENESS IS A LEARNED SKILL.

Forgiveness is a learned skill that improves with practice, and you'll soon see the benefits. The sooner you forgive the person who hurts you, the sooner you can effectively deal with the action, even if that may take a while because stepfamily hurts go deep. You give yourself the time and space to deal with hurts when you make the choice to forgive quickly so the healing can begin.

Second, look at the whole picture. See the people in your life as the complicated individuals they are. They make poor choices sometimes. So do you. They have forces acting upon them that you may not see. There is usually more to every story than we know. It's not our place to judge, only to journey.

When we understand all we can, and then tap into our courage, we can be strong enough to forgive those who hurt us, because we *choose* to do so. We can look at our big, full lives and see where all the pieces, even the ugly and painful ones, fit so that we can build better lives from this day on.

Forgiving doesn't erase anything, but it reframes it. Before you forgive, the hurt controls you. Afterward, you control the next step. You're free to accept that person into your life, flaws and all. And most importantly, you regain control of yourself.

Create in me a clean heart, O God, and renew a steadfast spirit within me. Do not cast me away from Your presence, and do not take Your Holy Spirit from me.
—Psalm 51:10–11 (NKJV)

Forgiving doesn't make you a victim, but chaining yourself to someone else's mistakes or attacks does. Your life is so much more than a fight with your stepkids' mom or a hateful stepchild. You are bigger than all of that when you forgive so you can repair the damage, when you focus less on their actions and more on your reaction.

No, it won't be quick, most likely, and you'll have days when you'll think forgiveness is impossible. But it comes when you allow it, when you choose to "clean" that hurting spot on your heart and leave the everyday pain and that increasingly heavy grudge behind.

THE GIFT IT BRINGS

So does your forgiveness give those who hurt you a "free pass" to do it again? No, because people do what they please with or without your blessing. But it gives *you* permission to feel whole again. As long as you hold on to a hurt, you aren't whole, and you know that you can't face any day as a stepmom if you're missing anything! Stepfamily troubles require your complete focus and attention—and a strength that comes from the power of forgiveness. You're doing yourself the biggest favor of all when you forgive.

THE DESIRE TO DO IT

Finally, you need to *want* to forgive. You need to want to get past the pain more than you want to avenge it, to care more about healing than reliving the past. Just think about the Lord's reaction to us when we need forgiveness. He doesn't have to forgive us, but He does, because He *wants* to. Surely, we can strive to behave in this same manner.

> *Let the wicked forsake his way, and the unrighteous man his thoughts; let him return to the LORD, and He will have mercy on him; and to our God, for He will abundantly pardon.*
>
> —*Isaiah 55:7 (NKJV)*

To Think About _____

Take your time to complete answers to each of the following questions.

What is the hardest part for you in learning the skill of forgiveness?

Can you mimic God's grace and feel His love in at least one hurt today?

Describe the change in your heart.

How will granting forgiveness to those who hurt you bring you the gift of healing and hope?

If you and your stepkids' mom can practice forgiveness between each other, imagine what a beautiful example of God's grace that will give your kids!

To God in Prayer

Lord, please help me see the great value in following Your example and forgiving those who hurt me. I want to feel whole, healed, and happy again, and I can't when the hurts are haunting me. Please show me how to respond as You would, how to forgive, and how to forge ahead. Amen.

God's Response

If God encouraged you in some specific way, use this space to record His response.

CHAPTER FIFTEEN

LEARNING TO ACCEPT

For no other foundation can anyone lay than that which is laid, which is Jesus Christ.

—1 Corinthians 3:11 (NKJV)

*A*s we work through the problems in our stepfamilies, we realize that we can beat our heads against the wall over and over and over—forever—if we want to do so. That wall will be there, just because it is. The other choice is to learn first to accept the wall and everything that goes with it, and then to work within ourselves to deal with it more effectively. The Lord knows when our issues are complicated and heavy, and He will walk with us to a solution.

ACCEPTANCE, NOT DEFEAT

We can spend a lot of time trying to win, if we want to. But we'll find only aggravation and disappointment because you can't always "win" in a stepfamily saga. Even when you do win, sometimes the price is too high. On the other hand, we tend to bristle at the idea of accepting whatever is thrown at us and letting others rule our lives. There is a solution, though, where we are neither defeated nor damaged.

Through the LORD's mercies we are not consumed, because His compassions fail not. They are new every morning; great is Your faithfulness.

—*Lamentations 3:22–23 (NKJV)*

When we accept the situations for what they are, then we can begin to work within them with the power we have. You may not like the way your husband relates to his former wife, but once you accept his choices, you can make your own. Instead of fighting what he's doing (with possibly poor results), you can focus on what *you* will do.

> *B*ECAUSE YOU CAN'T CONTROL OTHERS, YOU BENEFIT WHEN YOU USE YOUR ENERGY FOR CONTROLLING YOURSELF.

Because you can't control others, you benefit when you use your energy for controlling yourself. Will this approach always get you what you want? No, nothing will, but it will move your agenda to one you can create and change.

Should you still look for compromise and improvement? Absolutely. Accepting a fact doesn't condone it—it simply gets you from the complaining stage to the action stage. You start looking for how you'll adapt to the situation, what you'll change, or what you'll do to make things better for yourself, and that leads to a feeling of power and accomplishment. You don't feel victimized or defeated anymore, but a part of the solution instead, even if everything you can do is only about *you*.

Teach me to do your will, for you are my God; may your good Spirit lead me on level ground.

—*Psalm 143:10 (NIV)*

What to Do When You Can't Accept

What about the situations that are completely unacceptable? Are there ever any of those? Of course there are. If you have children of your own and they're being abused, ridiculed, or harmed in any way as part of your stepfamily, you can't accept that. If you are being subjected to behavior from your husband, stepkids, or their mom that is damaging your physical or mental health, you can't accept that either. These situations call for radical change.

When Jesus overturned the tables in the temple (John 2:15), He was calling for radical change. Sometimes, you may have to overturn some tables too. If so, do it with God at your side, knowing that He will show you what you need to do so that your actions reflect your acceptance of *His* ways into your life first.

Your Biggest Acceptance Challenge

Beyond the specific situations you'll either accept or reject, you'll make perhaps the most important choice in the part your stepkids will play in your life. Will you accept them completely into your home and heart? Often, that answer is determined by them, if they reject you or their dad. But when the choice of acceptance is completely yours, you hold the power of your relationship's future.

You've often read that you don't have to love your stepkids. That's true. You don't even have to like them. But accepting them as a part of your life can come first, and that makes everything easier in three ways.

1. We love what we claim. Once you claim your stepkids as a part of your life, you allow yourself to look at them differently. No longer are they your husband's kids, but *your family*. No, they won't suddenly be perfect, but neither is the rest of your world. Once you accept the kids as flawed beings—just like the rest of us—you open your heart and feelings of attachment grow.

2. You have an ally. When you accept your stepkids into your life, you have a kinship with them. It's not by blood, but by choice. And just like that, you're all on the same side. You begin to look for solutions that are best for everyone. The kids are not your competition but your comrades.

3. *Your goals keep pace with your choice.* Your goals need to reflect your whole life. When you accept your life as one that includes stepkids forever, you can factor them into your goals. Again, we can deal with anything if we understand it enough and when we choose it. As you work to fully welcome your stepkids into your life and heart, not just on the surface, but completely, you can adapt your goals to that choice. Your goals won't be weaker; they'll just reflect your changing life.

> *The Lord will fulfill his purpose for me; your love,*
> *O Lord endures forever—do not abandon the works of your*
> *hands.*
>
> *—Psalm 138:8 (NIV)*

Sometimes, we fight the full acceptance of things around us, believing that others will view us as a weak victim who is afraid to stand up for herself. But it will not be that way if we make the first move. Accept the people you want to love into your life, accept the choices of others, and live your role as stepmom the way you want, the way that glorifies God, and the way that helps you build a lasting family.

To Think About _____

Take your time to complete answers to each of the following questions.

What idea of acceptance have you had in the past?

Can you look at acceptance in a new way and start today to live the life you want, by your choice?

What does God want you to accept so that you can reach your goals?

What progress can you make today?

To God in Prayer

Lord, please help me accept all that You have prepared for me. Please help me accept others and their places in my life. Help me hear Your words to direct me in all the choices I have to make, and help me accept my stepmother role as a gift from You. Amen.

God's Response

If God encouraged you in some specific way, use this space to record His response.

A Stepmom Prays . . .

I am proud to be a stepmom. I've been in this role for almost three years. I look back on how much I've learned. As I look forward, I know I will learn so much more!

One of the most challenging aspects of being a stepmom is dealing with the kids' mom. Well-meaning friends and family "warned" me about her domineering and inconsiderate personality, and some even said I would naturally have to defer to her lead as far as the kids were concerned. I listened, pondered, and decided to take my own route: to be myself and to be the mom in my house. That is a liberating feeling! Easier said than done.

I started out with expectations that I would receive mutual respect from the mom since I, too, cared for and loved our kids. This expectation was dashed one summer day two years ago when the mom provoked me into a nasty verbal altercation. I actually don't feel guilty about anything I said, as I retained as much dignity and composure as I could muster during such an intensely stressful situation. The thing I regret is our daughter witnessed some of the argument, and I know it affected her view of us.

After the bad scene, which left me shaken both mentally and emotionally, I evaluated my own actions and how I should proceed in the future with this difficult person in my life. Since that incident, I have worked hard to remain positive to the kids about their mom at all times. I also refrain from saying negative things about her to my husband, as I don't believe in bringing up unpleasant topics (her!) unless it's necessary.

The kids' mom continues to this day to be difficult and tries her best to interfere in our lives and our household. We've had to change the way we do things now and then to show her we have made healthy boundaries around our family time with the kids and our physical property. Our motto is to remain steady and calm and to do what is best for the kids and everyone involved.

She and I rarely see other. When we do at soccer games or a recital, I say hello and sometimes how are you. This has helped me regain confidence and poise in front of her. I won't kid you, though. I still get queasy when I know I have to be in the same room with her.

In the past two years, I have grown tremendously as a person and as a stepmom. When things get out of balance or if the mom inserts herself unnecessarily in my home life, I remember to be myself, which allows me confidence that I can handle any situation she throws at me, and I know *I* am Mom in my house.

—**Liza** from Missouri

Peace in Coping

You'll learn to cope with your steplife, either in a positive or negative way. So will everyone around you. And sometimes you'll see how everything's going in the most surprising of ways.

On a damp Saturday morning, my husband and I met my stepson's mom at the soccer field. Many kicks and falls and a few raindrops later, the game was over. My stepson was going home with his mom that day, and as we all dashed to our vehicles, from under the raincoat before he climbed in his mom's car, my stepson waved at us and called, "'Bye, love you both!" No hesitation, no fear, just matter of fact. No doubt at many soccer fields that morning, little boys and girls worried about their parents' comments or actions, parents shot dirty looks or maybe even angry words at one another, and the air breathed hostility back at all who breathed it in. But for our family, it was another day of coping with the life we led. Simply that and nothing more. It's been years since that cool fall morning, but it's a memory I cherish, because at least for that unexpected moment, we could all know we'd done our best, and we could trust that to be enough.

Growing

"He looks on the earth, and it trembles; He touches the hills, and they smoke.
I will sing to the Lord as long as I live; I will sing praise to my God while I have my being.
May my meditation be sweet to Him; I will be glad in the Lord."

—Psalm 104:32–34(NKJV)

Growing Issues for the Life and Times of a Stepmom

- *Joy*
- *Release*
- *Insight*
- *Perspective*
- *Gratitude*

Growing

We begin our steplives in hope and quickly find ourselves deep in prayer as a necessity, unable to do much more. Then, as we work through the troubles of the role, we find ourselves deep in prayer as a *habit*, a delicious and wonderful habit that brings God to us every second.

We begin to know Him intimately, especially when He heals the wounds of steplife and shows us how to be the person He wants us to be, not in spite of, but because of our role as a step-mom. We begin to realize how much He loves us and wants to be with us, as difficult and imperfect as we are! We get a glimpse of the life and plan He has for us, and we find a reason to hope again, to believe in the future we can build.

All of our growth is not without some growing pains, though. We pay the price, fight the battles, question our sanity, and feel like giving up—a lot—but God never does. He stays close and every time we go to Him, He shows us a way around the hurt. We learn to adapt to the change in our world, and we learn how to appreciate all God has given us. We learn to work in our own hearts *first* to create the life we want.

We grow in our relationship with the Lord, and through that, everything else grows too. We develop a new way of looking at our whole lives, through the heart and grace of God. We still have growing to do, but we've learned the best way to do anything: holding hands with God, because He always knows where we are going.

Chapter Sixteen

Expecting Joy

*Be glad in the Lord and rejoice, you righteous; and shout
for joy, all you upright in heart!*

—Psalm 32:11 (NKJV)

*B*ecause stepfamilies that survive are stepfamilies of
choice, there has to be a lot of joy seeping out between the
edges. Even if the family still reels now and then from steplife
fallout, you can still find joy when it's tied to your growth in
Christ.

The joy that decorates your life isn't a fleeting moment
of pleasure, but a deep and abiding trust in God and great
thankfulness that He has led you this far—over a thousand
landmines—to the security only He provides.

A Heart of Joy

We all know that feeling of joy when a stepchild loves out of
choice, when our family is whole and strong, when God is near
and we can feel Him. The trick is in holding on to that joy deep
in our hearts when chaos reigns above. And it's important that
we do, because the result affects everything else.

"The good man brings good things out of the good stored up in his heart. . . . For out of the overflow of his heart his mouth speaks."

—*Luke 6:45 (NIV)*

With your growing relationship and interaction with God, you can speak joy to all those around you because He has filled your heart with an abundance of it. Joy is in the strength of your marriage and the way you've learned to live your stepmom role. Life is not perfect, but it's not far from it all the time either. Joy is in your reconciliation of all that's unfair and your victory over all that has hurt you. It's in your deep trust in God, because the two of you have been through quite a bit since you signed up for this life challenge!

> *W*E FEEL THE JOY THAT A WALK WITH GOD BRINGS.

When the times are especially difficult, we find great solace in our retreats to God and in all that He teaches us. That closeness makes our hearts a little lighter, because we feel the joy that a walk with God brings, despite the conditions we may have to slosh through now and then. We apply that feeling to everything around us, and we find more joy awaits.

There is deceit in the hearts of those who plot evil, but joy for those who promote peace.

—*Proverbs 12:20 (NIV)*

OUR FOCUS

When we aren't trying to control or manipulate those around us, but only uphold and encourage instead, the joy in our hearts shows itself, in our voice, and in our choice. Using our great relationship with God as a pattern, we learn how to seek and find even more joy because we know where to look. We don't let the temporary problems of the day erode the lasting progress we've made, and that fact alone is cause for celebration. We get much better at this practice as we mature as a stepmom.

We can't fight or even try to fix everything all the time, but we can frame everything we need to do in the knowledge of the Lord's love and devotion to us. If we continue to look there first, we remember who holds us always, and that is a joy no problem can quiet.

Joy Unexpected

When we're in the trenches of tough steplife troubles, we often ask why and how this could be happening to us. We may think of the stepchild who rejects us or belittles us as punishment. But God sees it all as fodder for our growth, a way to a joy that lasts when the pain is gone.

> *Now no chastening seems to be joyful for the present, but painful; nevertheless, afterward it yields the peaceable fruit of righteousness to those who have been trained by it.*
> —*Hebrews 12:11 (NKJV)*

The joy that you never expect to find is one of the greatest. It's the joy of overcoming a loss, of solving a problem, of even being convicted by God to learn something you've neglected to learn so far. Of course, the steplife traumas are exhausting, but they're not bigger than knowing the joy of a God-filled life, or of the satisfaction that comes from becoming a better stepmom as a result of them.

Truly, we can bank on the Lord creating joy for us even when we doubt we'll ever see any again! Problems come with a guarantee. If we meet them, they will serve us. We may not know how right away, but they will. And in that knowledge and trust, we find joy. Regardless of the chaos around us or the pain within us, we can rest in the promise of something far better yet to come from God who is supporting us.

> *But the fruit of the Spirit is love, joy, peace, patience, kindness, goodness, faithfulness, gentleness and self-control.*
>
> —*Galatians 5:22–23 (NIV)*

JOY IN THE JOURNEY

The Lord delights in bringing joy into our lives. He smiles with us at the thought of our blessed hearts and inspired spirits. And that joy is everywhere we look when our focus is on God for each step. It's a joy in the journey.

With questions of wonder, we prepare ourselves for the joy: *What does He want me to see here? What blessing might be hidden, just waiting for me to receive it here? How will I receive this experience into my life and find the joy within it here?*

This approach shows us that real joy isn't a slice of luck, but a pervasive attitude that creates its own happiness, always here, no matter what. Joy is a belief in God's goodness and trust in His plans, even when we don't always feel the obvious and immediate effects. It's found in the survival of an encounter with your stepkids' mom, in your choice for a better reaction and a search for a solution—perhaps something you might not have always been able to achieve.

When we learn how to find joy in our lives this way, we learn so much more. We often learn how to avoid the absence of it in the first place. Simple pleasures in a stepmom's life can be quite limited at first. But as we grow, we learn to latch on to them whenever we can, and we learn what impedes them.

Maybe we know that a certain topic with a stepteen is always trouble, so we choose our times for talking carefully or learn to temper our comments. And when a moment of joy presents itself, we drink that up and resist the urge to make a point or further a discussion that might kill it and lead to harsh words. Something as simple as a shared bowl of cereal without the expectation of anything else can give us a moment of joy to be remembered, a breather, and a smile to help sustain us in the not-so-joyous times.

If we allow these moments to come without conflict, they accumulate and help fill our hearts with joy to brighten our outlook on everything else. When we learn to censor ourselves in those delicate interactions that can sap all the energy from our souls, we hold on to the joy even longer. It's all about paying attention to each opportunity.

The little things *do* matter the most, and they add up to so much more than we think they ever will. Our tender Lord provides them for us daily if we only look.

 To Think About _____

Take your time to complete answers to each of the following questions.

Where do you find the greatest joys in your life?

Where do you find joy in your role as stepmom?

How does your growing relationship with the Lord bring you more joy daily?

What have you learned to avoid so that you have more joy and less heartache?

To God in Prayer

Lord, thank You for the joy of being Your child, in knowing that You will always help and guide me and show me amazing gifts as I work to become a successful stepmom. Please help me become aware of Your touch, hear Your words, and never miss a single joy You want me to have. Amen.

God's Response

If God encouraged you in some specific way, use this space to record His response.

CHAPTER SEVENTEEN

EXPERIENCING SWEET RELEASE

Therefore, if anyone is in Christ, he is a new creation; old things have passed away; behold, all things have become new.

—2 Corinthians 5:17 (NKJV)

*D*espite our best efforts, we make lots of mistakes as stepmoms. Even after many years, we still feel twinges of jealousy or react out of fear. We are generally pretty hard on ourselves when something such as that happens, when it feels as if we erase all of our progress with a few poor choices.

But God says no. He says that we can have release from everything that hurts; and with His help, we grow to understand how.

RELEASE FROM THE PAST

Sometimes, we feel like the life before this one just won't let go! The old wounds still hurt and influence how we act today. We try to move on, but it's hard. We learn quickly, though, that living in the past won't do anything to help the present, and it can certainly affect the future.

The Lord has a bountiful future for you planned and waiting. All of the time you spend looking back takes away from time you could be using to go forward. The choice is yours, but God has a preference.

When we choose to release the past and stop letting it dictate our future, then the present gets much clearer. That's because the past, full of aches, disappointments, and mistakes, is like a giant mountain we can't see around. If we want to see around it, we have to stop looking at it and look at God instead. Then reflected back to us is the picture of a stepmom atop the mountain, still capable and strong, one who can let go of the past because she trusts God to hold the future.

> *THE LORD HAS A BOUNTIFUL FUTURE FOR YOU PLANNED AND WAITING.*

And she trusts God to hold *her*— flawed and needy, still learning and growing every day. When we allow ourselves to release the past, we release so much more, and our growth accelerates to heights unimagined.

> *Those who are planted in the house of the LORD shall flourish in the courts of our God. They shall still bear fruit in old age; they shall be fresh and flourishing.*
> —*Psalm 92:13–14 (NKJV)*

RELEASING MORE

Along with our own mistakes, we need to release others from our expectations and dependencies. When we do that, we then hold on to them, not with a chokehold but with a warm embrace. We look to ourselves for answers and to God for guidance, and from that steady place, we are strong enough to face a distant stepchild without a crutch of an unhappy past. Instead, you release him and yourself to pursue something that will work, to come together when you can to forge something new every day, in every situation.

You are strong enough to love without demanding love in return, to give without expecting glory. When you release those you love from an obligation to perform, you stop looking at their reactions. You make better choices for *your* actions based on what matters to you because you are redeemed and can in great joy "put on the new self, created to be like God in true righteousness and holiness" (Ephesians 4:24 NIV).

GATHERING CLOSE

The Lord trusts us enough to offer His grace and then wait for us to call Him close. If we'll release everything that we've parked in the way between Him and us, we can bring Him closer. You will hear His wisdom when you start to dwell on a comment your stepkids' mom made five years ago. You will feel His gentle push away from what drives danger into your steplife and toward reconciliation and regeneration instead.

> *It is God who works in you to will and act according to his good purpose.*
> —Philippians 2:13 (NIV)

When we release the past that hurts and the present that hinders, we are free to grow, to explore untapped areas of our stepmother-hood—things we couldn't see before because we weren't looking at God first. When we let the Lord release us from what blocks our view, we have a new view of our value to Him and to our family. We can focus on becoming the stepmom we want to be and let go of everything that gets in our way.

To Think About _____

Take your time to complete answers to each of the following questions.

What do you need to release today?

What can you release others from so that healing can begin?

How will you keep the past in the past and focus on the future God has planned for you?

To God in Prayer

L ord, please help me release everything damaging that I hold so tightly in my heart. I pray for Your wisdom and direction as You hold me close so that I can focus on You and our future. Please help me hold You and my loved ones just as close. Amen.

God's Response

If God encouraged you in some specific way, use this space to record His response.

Chapter Eighteen

Gaining Insight

The Lord will guide you always; he will satisfy your needs in a sun-scorched land and will strengthen your frame. You will be like a well-watered garden, like a spring whose waters never fail.

—Isaiah 58:11 (NIV)

*F*ew experiences are the education that a stepfamily is! The discoveries about ourselves, those around us, and even God occur daily. For a while, we don't know how to make much of it all, and we're too stressed to want to in some cases. But eventually, as the Lord keeps talking to us and we keep working, we develop a keen insight into the world in which we live.

Do we have all the answers and explanations for everything after a few years? Hardly! But we do learn to build on what we know, sort of like a detective with many years of experience. Along with the comfort that comes with time, we are intimately aware of the tiny nuances of our stepmotherhood.

We learn to "read" the situations we face with a much keener eye. We realize that our starting point for dealing with an issue becomes about 20 paces ahead of what it used to be. Our well-deserved insight is no coincidence. It is one of God's blessings as we grow, both as His disciple and as a stepmom.

Be very careful, then, how you live—not as unwise but as wise,
making the most of every opportunity.
           —Ephesians 5:15–16 (NIV)

For example, your run-ins with your stepkids' mom may have almost destroyed you in the beginning. You may have reacted without thinking, only in pain and anger. As the Lord works through you, though, you learn to react with your mind first instead of your heart. You learn what works, and you quit beating yourself up with what doesn't. You can size up a threat and form a plan almost instantly. You have learned much because you had to, and it all started with your quest for peace in your life.

> YOU LEARN TO REACT WITH YOUR MIND FIRST INSTEAD OF YOUR HEART.

Insight and Relief

You may be surprised to know this, but your prayer for insight *improves* your insight before God even intervenes, because looking for insight is the first step. Here's how.

When we pray for insight into how to make our lives better, we're looking for resolution, not retaliation. We're operating out of grace, not greed. We're acknowledging that there is much we don't know, and we are open to receive. As we go to God with this lack, we find abundance. He demonstrates it all as He teaches us about *Him*. And if we choose to learn and follow, we are forever changed.

We cry for help to work through all the mess before us, and He reminds us that He is in control. We ask for relief from the confusion, and He reminds us where our direction is found. We ask to know what we don't see, and He reminds us that He knows everything, and that He will not abandon our hearts as we search for answers.

*For God is greater than our hearts, and he knows
everything.*

—1 John 3:20 (NIV)

As we work from a belief in what the Lord tells us in response
to our questions, our insight grows as we grow closer to Him.
Our trust in Him and confidence that He has hold of everything
gives us the ability to see what we missed before. With God in
control, we are not afraid to look directly into the many complications of our life and see beyond the obvious.

Every new problem isn't something that scares us to death
anymore. As we practice what He preaches to us, we learn to
investigate before we scream, to see the whole road before us
instead of just the latest bump, to reflect on what we've learned
and apply it to today.

Insight Tested

Every bit of insight we gain is based on our faith. We grow when
we trust that God is in control, that He is directing our paths,
and that He will show us the "something more" we need to
know now. When we face the rebellious stepchild or her vindic-
tive mom, we can approach the situation with God at our side—
looking for answers and explanations, knowing how to assess the
facts and respond accordingly—because we have learned from
the One who is afraid of nothing. "Who has preceded Me, that
I should pay him? Everything under heaven is Mine" (Job 41:11
NKJV).

We also realize, as much as we wish it weren't so, that there
will be situations we can't explain or solve, but our trust in God
grants us insight to see what we *can* do, to spend our energy
in the right places. Continually pushing yourself on a stepchild
who resists may be a poor choice. Your insight, which increases
every day, will provide you with another solution. For example,
you may write letters about how you feel and give them to your

stepchild when he is grown. Sometimes, we have to change our approach and make tough choices, and we learn that we can.

Trusting God and using His teachings as an example gives you the insight to make those choices, that "your heart may be enlightened in order that you may know the hope to which he has called you" (Ephesians 1:18 NIV).

He never abandons us as we work through the difficult issues we face. He guides us to find the answers we can use. Our trust in Him grows with every turn we make to Him, and our insight into better managing our role grows at the same time. We see so much more clearly every time we look to God first, and we know that He sees all.

To Think About _____

Take your time to complete answers to each of the following questions.

How has your insight into your role changed over time?

How has your insight improved in the delicate relationship with your stepkids' mom, and what have you learned?

If you still feel lost and confused, how can you apply the Lord's guarantees to your situation?

What one area will you work in first to gain valuable insight?

How will you rely on your faith to help you?

To God in Prayer

Lord, please grant me the ability to look beyond what is obvious, to see what others see, to respond with answers and actions worthy of You. I pray for insight that shows me more of You and Your plans so that I may live my life reflective of You. Please show me the best choices I can make. Amen.

God's Response

If God encouraged you in some specific way, use this space to record His response.

CHAPTER NINETEEN

LOOKING AHEAD

For we are God's workmanship, created in Christ Jesus to do good works, which God prepared in advance for us to do.

—Ephesians 2:10 (NIV)

Few things in life can make you lose your perspective more than becoming a stepmom, wouldn't you agree? Everything becomes a crisis, and we can easily lose sight of what matters most. We're so busy treading water that we become engulfed by every little wave. Then after wasting precious time in the struggle, we realize that we're getting no closer to our destination.

The Lord reminds us every now and then to settle down and adopt His perspective for our stepmom issues—and everything else.

But those who wait on the LORD shall renew their strength; they shall mount up with wings like eagles, they shall run and not be weary, they shall walk and not faint.

—Isaiah 40:31 (NKJV)

By following the Lord's lead, we are able to do two things: we can hold out for the good we trust is yet to come, and we can avoid the depression that comes with an obsession over the bad.

LOOKING FAR AHEAD

When we practice a long-range perspective, like God's, we can trust that everything difficult is temporary, that the poor attitude of a teenager isn't our fault, that the interference of her mom will come to an end one day.

> *WITH THAT POSITIVE PERSPECTIVE, YOU ARE A STEPMOM WITH POWER.*

When we look beyond the troubles of the moment, we gain great inspiration and determination, and even a little patience. And sometimes, just focusing on good times to come gives our hearts enough of a rest to get us through the tough times. Our minds are clearer, too, when we focus on the guaranteed peace yet to come as much as we focus on the present difficulty.

> *Finally, brothers, whatever is true, whatever is noble, whatever is right, whatever is pure, whatever is lovely, whatever is admirable—if anything is excellent or praiseworthy—think about such things.*
>
> —Philippians 4:8 (NIV)

By looking with that perspective, our minds begin to believe that a solution will be found for every problem, that we only have to flesh out what our hearts have already decided: that no obstacle is insurmountable and no difficulty is beyond our strength.

LOOKING WITH POWER

With that positive perspective, you are a stepmom with power.

Battles with stepkids are a detour, not the whole journey. Your marriage is the path of your life now, and while it includes a role as stepmom, it is still the anchor for everything else, and when you remember and hold on to that, despite a few storms, you develop an attitude—a perspective—of confidence and resolve.

If you're bogged down by every steplife tragedy, large and small, you lose ground that's hard to make up. The grip on a perspective of continual hope and God's eternal wisdom keeps us going and allows the joy we desperately need to filter unbidden into our lives.

> *Therefore, my dear brothers, stand firm. Let nothing move you. Always give yourselves fully to the work of the Lord, because you know that your labor in the Lord is not in vain.*
>
> *—1 Corinthians 15:58 (NIV)*

A perspective that looks at tests with great faith insulates us from the debilitating emotions of anger and hurt. It's not an attempt to whitewash the issues you face, but instead, to prevent them from becoming all you see.

While the disruptive or manipulative stepchild who refuses to obey you is certainly cause for concern, a clear perspective will prevent the situation from destroying you. By seeing the problem as one issue and not a prediction of the rest of your life, you can deal with it more effectively. By isolating your hurt, you keep it in check, segregated and not all-encompassing. You trust that a solution is coming. You go to the Lord expecting to find answers, and He never fails to deliver.

> *Let us then approach the throne of grace with confidence, so that we may receive mercy and find grace to help us in our time of need.*
>
> *—Hebrews 4:16 (NIV)*

By refusing to allow the challenges to appear bigger than they are, you can keep everything in its place, everything in a true perspective. Yes, the former wife who calls too often is annoying, but it doesn't have to be all you think about unless you allow it to be. With a clear perspective, you can counter every problem with abundant conviction that you will overcome and be stronger because of it. The Lord planned it that way.

To Think About _____

Take your time to complete answers to each of the following questions.

What is your perspective of your stepfamily?

How has it changed over the years?

How can you claim the Lord's perspective to improve your outlook on your life?

What new perspective will help make your role easier?

To God in Prayer

L ord, please help me see beyond today, my immediate trouble, to see that You have everything in Your hands, and that nothing will come to pass that You cannot make good. Please help me find the calm and clarity of a clear perspective in every part of my steplife. Amen.

God's Response

If God encouraged you in some specific way, use this space to record His response.

CHAPTER TWENTY

GIVING GRATITUDE

But I will sing of Your power; yes, I will sing aloud of Your mercy in the morning; for you have been my defense and refuge in the day of my trouble. To You, O my Strength, I will sing praises; for God is my defense, the God of my mercy.

—*Psalm 59:16–18 (NKJV)*

We learn many things as stepmoms, but undoubtedly one of the most important is a spirit of gratitude. When we can give thanks daily, we can sustain almost any hit, because we've planted our hearts in God's bountiful garden.

Early in our lives as stepmoms, we are often faced with more reasons to complain than to compliment. We often deal with many takers and few givers, and almost no one can understand the depth of our pain.

So we cry out to God, and He answers, "I'm already here." Instantly, we feel rested and hopeful again. For that undeniable fact, we are grateful. It feels good to be thankful to God again.

You who have done great things; O God, who is like You?
You, who have shown me great and severe troubles, shall
revive me again, and bring me up again from the depths
of the earth. You shall increase my greatness, and comfort
me on every side.

—*Psalm 71:19–21 (NKJV)*

From that new beginning, we find our gratitude becoming more powerful each day. Because when we are thankful, we are not hurting. Our focus has shifted.

"Peace I leave with you, My peace I give to you; not as the
world gives do I give to you. Let not your heart be troubled,
neither let it be afraid.

—*John 14:27 (NJKV)*

If indeed the Lord has not abandoned us in our turmoil (even when we think He has), then surely He has sent us other blessings we've neglected to claim as well. As we go through our stepmom role, sometimes easily and sometimes with great difficulty, we learn to see these blessings and draw a quiet strength from them that is truly heaven-sent.

> WHEN WE
> ARE THANKFUL,
> WE ARE NOT
> HURTING.

When times are fairly uneventful and crises are at a minimum, be thankful for the respite. The Lord knows when to send us a break! During the times of quiet, take a moment to reconnect with God and remember where your spirit belongs, to give thanks for His care and nurture, to get in touch with the One who holds you close even when you're not paying attention.

Gratitude seems easy, and if it is, that's OK. It's great practice for the times when it doesn't seem so easy. The tough patches of steplife often send us searching for relief, rarely eager to offer gratitude. But when we realize that they're the same thing, we find more of those blessings our Lord has waiting.

WE ASK, HE GIVES

After a few seasons as a stepmom, we learn that when we hurt, we are better instantly when we thank God for His help and guidance yet to come, for how He will inspire and comfort us in our troubles, for His grasp on our hearts when our minds are too scattered to think. That gratitude as a first response is relief. It prepares us to receive all the love, care, and direction our Lord will faithfully supply, guaranteed.

> *"Ask, and it will be given to you; seek, and you will find; knock, and it will be opened to you. For everyone who asks receives, and he who seeks finds, and to him who knocks it will be opened."*
>
> *—Matthew 7:7–8 (NJKV)*

As we cultivate the habit of a grateful heart, we frame everything differently. When you can't connect with your stepchild, before you despair, thank God for the insights He will send your way, for the resolution He has already prepared. Then allow yourself to receive it.

Giving thanks out of habit for the basics leads us to realize that we already have what matters most—our ability to love and grow, our power of choice and resourcefulness in a challenging lifestyle, our relationship with God that is both the foundation and the sanctuary for everything that follows.

When we are mindful of God's generosity and compassion, we delight Him. If our heart is open to receive, there is no end to His care, and we all know how much care a stepmom needs!

Going to God with a grateful heart, we grant ourselves permission to be happy, despite steplife troubles. What we once viewed as a lack becomes just a fact sandwiched between blessings. With a faith we once thought inadequate, we depend on God to supply what we need, and He never fails.

In Abundance

> *"Take heed and beware of covetousness, for one's life does not consist in the abundance of the things he possesses."*
>
> Luke 12:15 (NKJV)

When we move our focus from things to thankfulness, we realize that we're most thankful for what possesses us—our God, our faith, our integrity, the Lord's grace that grants us this life to live for Him. When we live our lives every day for what possesses us, we see that the Lord's abundance fills up every ounce of our being.

A GRATEFUL HEART IS LIKE A WARM BLANKET.

A grateful heart is like a warm blanket. It wraps you in comfort, keeps away the harmful elements, and allows you to rest. Resting in God's blessings, we find enough to cover us completely, to meet the blows to our lives head-on, and win.

Giving thanks to God for what we have, what we've accomplished, and joys yet to appear, makes stepmothering easier, if only because we know we live this life with the Lord, in His graciousness, by our side.

 *To Think About* _____

Take your time to complete answers to each of the following questions.

Can you find plenty of reasons to be grateful to God, even with the complications of your stepfamily?

How have you failed to show your gratitude in the past, and how has that hurt you?

How will recognizing your blessings, now and those to come, make your life better?

What are you most grateful for as a stepmom?

To God in Prayer

Lord, thank You for being here with me, always, through the difficult and the delightful, the chaos and the calm. Thank You for always bringing the light to my darkness, and for granting me more blessings than I can ever count. Thank You for all the ways You will bless our family in the future. Thank You for everything. Amen.

God's Response

If God encouraged you in some specific way, use this space to record His response.

A Stepmom Prays . . .

I've prayed to God on numerous occasions, asking for help when neither my husband nor I would see eye to eye on issues regarding our children. He felt I was harder on his two children than I was with my son, and I felt it was the other way around.

God helped me realize I needed to step back to view the situation differently, to look through my husband's eyes and see his point of view. This helped tremendously, and once my husband realized I supported his decisions, he then supported mine.

We may not always see eye to eye on everything, but thanks to God, we've taken a different approach, which has a more positive outcome.

—**Kimberly**, stepmom of two, mom of one

A Stepmom Prays . . .

In a few months' time, two of our children, one daughter and one son, announced their engagements just three and a half weeks apart. Wow and double wow!

In preparation one day, we went to lunch at a local restaurant with my son (he is my stepson), his fiancée, my daughter (she is my stepdaughter), and my husband, Moe's, former wife, her husband, and their two children. This was a first for us. When I arrived, Moe was not there yet. I was there by myself with his former wife and her family. Yikes! My stomach rolled!

I remember sitting at a rehearsal dinner where four sets of parents were giving each other the "eyes" as they tried to outdo the other with toasts to the bride and groom. At the wedding, things became so stressful and uncomfortable that the bride and groom left the reception (with the groom in tears) 45 minutes early without telling their guests good-bye. I didn't want a repeat of this scene at my son's wedding.

So, how did we get through that lunch and many to come?

Prayer. It really works. I prayed for peaceful encounters throughout the entire wedding planning and pre-events. I continued to pray for "the day." Putting aside our feelings and misgivings, and swallowing our pride. It hurts, but it is worth it.

Making an effort. Sometimes our first step may be small, but before we know it, we are walking full stride. The first step is hard, but just as a baby's first steps turn to a run, we will be running soon too.

So how did our lunch turn out? We all sat at the same table (Moe finally arrived) calmly, without harsh words, stress, or bad vibes. We worked through the details of the rehearsal dinner together. Moe's former spouse and I were smiling, talking, working together, even talking about what color dresses we would wear. As we were walking to our cars, Cricket turned to say good-bye. Her name is no longer "Moe's former wife." She didn't seem so bad after all.

I knew my son was going to have a great wedding.

—**Paige Becnel,** mother of two, stepmother of three

A Stepmom Prays . . .

Prayer and my relationship with Jesus are vital to my ability to press on despite the obstacles I face as a stepmother. I don't even want to imagine how difficult steplife would be without prayer! I cling to Philippians 4:6–8, and I find so much encouragement in those words. I don't consider any concern of mine too petty to take to the Lord in prayer, and I try to focus not on the hurts and setbacks of steplife, but rather on the joys and triumphs, no matter how seemingly minor.

When I pray for my stepfamily, I thank God for the struggles He has taken our family through, and I thank Him for the love, the grace, and the mercy He has modeled for us. I pray for wisdom, patience, compassion, and understanding. I pray that God will help me to accept the situations and actions that are out of my control and to release my expectations and assumptions about how and when our stepfamily should blend.

I pray for strength, guidance, and the heart to persevere in the midst of challenges. And I pray for my husband, my stepson and his mother, and our family as a whole so that we can overcome those challenges together, grow closer to one another, and be witnesses for Jesus, through whom we can do all things.

I'm grateful that we are blessed and don't have many of the same problems that other stepfamilies have (for example, my husband and I have an amiable relationship with my stepson's mom, and our daughter and her big brother adore each other), but we still struggle with different discipline styles, expectations, and communication skills. Just when I think we're starting to make progress on something, my stepson is gone again, and when he returns, he seems to have forgotten where we left off. Prayer is the most powerful parenting implement in my toolbox, though, and the progress that results from prayer is long lasting.

—**Shauna**, stepmom of one, mommy of one

Peace in Growing

Getting to the growing part of stepmotherhood is a joy, but it doesn't come easy. It means lots of work along the way, and then finally, you can relax a bit. You can trust that while you'll still never get it right all the time, some things are OK.

When my older stepson turned 21, we planned a little party, just lots of food and some friends at home. I decided to invite my stepson's mom and stepdad too. We don't really socialize together, and I didn't know if they'd accept, but they did. And the world didn't split in two or anything—we were all together to celebrate our son's birthday and nothing more.

The presents were a big hit, we all ate too much, and I only had to clean up one spilled soda. And for my stepson, his "broken" home was filled with all his parents, and while he had grown up, so had we. We had all figured out a way to make it work, to overcome the past, to keep growing for everyone's sake.

The party we shared was just one evening, but it was one thing that was OK. It was peace grown from pain and well worth everything it took to get us there.

The best is always yet to be.

A STEPMOM'S PRAYER FOR PEACE

Now may the Lord of peace himself give you peace at all times and in every way.
                                        —*2 Thessalonians 3:16 (NIV)*

*P*erhaps of all a stepmom prays for, the greatest request is for *peace*. A troubled family can threaten even the most centered stepmom's feeling of peace, and a cry for the Lord's care is a daily practice. And He always responds because "the peace of God, which surpasses all understanding, will guard your hearts and minds through Christ Jesus" (Philippians 4:7 NKJV).

We start to find the peace we need when we recall our lives before stepmotherhood, before we had to adapt to a changing world we can never control. When we look back to who we were before, we see the child of God, untouched by the challenges of raising someone else's children.

And we reclaim her, that child God held closely, and we let Him do it again. We return to Him and start there, trusting Him for the peace only He can give in *any* kind of life. We trust that He will show us how to have the peaceful life we need, and in that trust, we learn something very important.

Even if we get everyone to do what we want, if we turn our stepkids into angels and their mom into a saint, it won't bring the real peace we crave unless *our* center is in God. Peace isn't about everyone doing the right things, but about us going right to God with the things just as they are. Anyone can be peaceful if nothing is wrong. We need to be at peace in the midst of a great many things that may be wrong.

> *"The LORD bless you and keep you; the LORD make his face shine upon you, and be gracious to you; the LORD lift up His countenance upon you, and give you peace."*
> —*Numbers 6:24–26 (NKJV)*

Only the Lord can save our spirit so that we can deal with a family where no angels reside. Only He enables us to claim a steady faith that gets us through every crisis—still intact. It is the peace we must have within *ourselves* that stems from that centering on God. It's a promise: "You will keep him in perfect peace, whose mind is stayed on You, because he trusts in You" (Isaiah 26:3 NKJV).

We can have that peace, regardless of whatever anyone else is doing, despite others' choices and actions. Our peace is not about the absence of error in our lives, but the presence of God in our lives. When we know that we've done our best, that we've responded with integrity and empathy, that we've met others with fairness and respect, then we have the lasting peace that comes from within.

Strangely enough, the trials of steplife will inspire us to that behavior because we recognize a better life when we see it. And the better life is one of *peace within ourselves* first, granted and guarded by God Almighty.

For I know the thoughts that I think toward you, says the Lord, thoughts of peace and not of evil, to give you a future and a hope. Then you will call upon Me and go and pray to me, and I will listen to you. And you will seek Me and find Me, when you search for Me with all your heart.

—Jeremiah 29:11–13 (NKJV)

My Prayer for You

I ask the Lord to watch over you and keep you close, to bring you joy and grant you an everlasting peace, to comfort you and make you strong. I thank Him for all the blessings He will pour upon you, for all the ways He will fill your heart, for all the steps He will make right beside you. May you find inspiration and direction in His words and His presence. May you find abundant happiness and peace in all you do, dear stepmom. In Jesus's name. Amen.

New Hope® Publishers is a division of WMU®,
an international organization
that challenges Christian believers
to understand and be radically involved in God's mission.
For more information about WMU, go to www.wmu.com.
More information about New Hope books may be found
at www.newhopepublishers.com. New Hope books
may be purchased at your local bookstore.

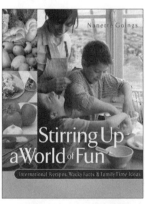